Three Plays After

Brian Friel was born in Omagh, County Tyrone, in 1929. His plays include *Philadelphia, Here I Come!*, *Translations*, *Making History* and *Dancing at Lughnasa*.

BRIAN FRIEL

Three Plays After

FARRAR, STRAUS AND GIROUX

NEW YORK

Farrar, Straus and Giroux
175 Varick Street, New York 10014

Copyright © 2001, 2002 by Brian Friel
All rights reserved
Printed in the United States of America
Originally published in 2002 by The Gallery Press
First published in this edition in 2002 by Faber and Faber Limited,
Great Britain
Published in the United States by Farrar, Straus and Giroux
First American edition, 2003

A CIP record for this book is available from the British Library
Paperback ISBN: 978-0-571-21761-8

Our books may be purchased in bulk for promotional, educational,
or business use. Please contact your local bookseller or the
Macmillan Corporate and Premium Sales Department at
1-800-221-7945, extension 5442, or by e-mail at
MacmillanSpecialMarkets@macmillan.com.

www.fsgbooks.com
www.twitter.com/fsgbooks • www.facebook.com/fsgbooks

P1

For Cassie

Contents

THE YALTA GAME

based on a theme in
The Lady with the Lapdog
by Anton Chekhov

The Yalta Game was first produced in the Gate Theatre, Dublin, on Tuesday, 2 October 2001, with the following cast:

Dmitry Dmitrich Gurov Ciarán Hinds
Anna Sergeyevna Kelly Reilly

Director Karel Reisz
Set Designer Eileen Diss
Costume Designer Dany Everett
Lighting Designer Mick Hughes
Composer Conor Linehan
Sound Designer John Leonard

Literal translation by Úna Ní Dhubhghaill

Characters

Dmitry Dmitrich Gurov

Anna Sergeyevna

Note

Dialogue **in bold type, thus,**
is between the characters.

Dialogue in roman type, thus,
is spoken to the audience.

The stage is furnished with a table with a circular, marble top; two or three chairs which can be used outdoors or indoors; and perhaps a couch.

Dmitry Dmitrich Gurov is thirty-nine. His hair is beginning to turn grey. He wears his straw hat at a jaunty angle and carries a cane. He is now enjoying the late summer sun in Yalta. An exuberant military band is playing in the distance. Gurov listens for a few moments.

GUROV Stirring, aren't they? Seventh Hussars from the camp over in Balaclava. (*He calls an imaginary waiter.*) **Another coffee when you find a second.** (*Listens to the music again and conducts vigorously.*) Make you want to charge into combat, wouldn't it?

The music begins to fade.

Believe me, when the summer season is at its height, there is no resort in the whole of the Crimea more exciting, more vibrant, than Yalta. The crowds. The bustling restaurants. The commotion of different languages. The promenade. The elegant municipal park. The obligatory day trip to the silver waterfall at Oreanda. The nightly ritual of going down to the quay and watching the new arrivals pouring out of the Theodosia ferry with its lights dancing and expectant. And of course the mysterious Black Sea itself that embraces and holds all these elements together, especially at night when the water is a soft, warm lilac and the moon throws a shaft of gold across it. (*to the imaginary waiter*) **Thank you kindly. And sugar? Excellent.** (*He now spreads out on a seat and tilts his*

7

straw hat forward so that his eyes are almost concealed.)
But of course the town square is the heart of Yalta.
That's where the tourists congregate and sip coffee from
morning until night. And from under their straw hats
and parasols, silently, secretly they scrutinize one
another. It is the great unacknowledged Yalta game. And
it is played in a kind of dream-state – and at the same
time almost voraciously.

(*softly*) That couple is back. Where were they yesterday?
Not married, are they? Madam, please! Certainly not
married. There's that Greek boy again. Still coughing.
His eyes are so disengaged – what disappointment is he
trying to recuperate from? When that husband dies this
winter, as indeed he will, what will become of her? Has
she the resolution to stagger on? Oh, yes, she has. Look
at her staring into space – she's already making all the
icy calculations.

They're new. French, are they? Has she been crying?
Haven't exchanged a word all afternoon. He's clearly a
prig. And his foot never stops tapping. Young lady, you
shouldn't let him see how desperately you love him.

It's a day-long diversion, drinking coffee and divining
other lives or investing the lives of others with an
imagined life. Harmless enough, I suppose.

Madam, please! This is a public square!

You know the season is coming to an end when you
see the first of the shutters going up and the wind whips
up a choking dust and there is only a score of coffee-
drinkers left to invent one another.

And slowly the vibrancy and excitement subside and
the place becomes . . . not yet desolate, but just a little
dejected. And you realize you have to disengage yourself
from these dreamy pleasures and this other-world routine
and think about going back to Moscow – work, children,
wife. (*Pause.*) Home. That requires a little . . . effort.

I had been in Yalta for almost two weeks and on my second-last day, about three in the afternoon, I was sitting in the square with the remnants of the faithful. And suddenly a young woman appeared. Out of the Marino Hotel. White blouse. Grey skirt. Simple little hat. And a fawn Pomeranian at her heels. And came across the square towards our corner, walking briskly with her head down as if she wanted to be under observation for as short a time as possible.

And the straw hats and parasols stirred ever so slightly.

Enter Anna Sergeyevna with her imaginary dog. She is twenty-two. She sits and calls a waiter.

ANNA **One coffee, please. Black.** (*to dog*) **Sit – sit.**

GUROV Now that's new. That's interesting. Twenty? Twenty-two? Not more. Russian? Oh yes. Married? Think so. Why? Instinct; and the dog maybe. Is there a husband back in the hotel? Maybe not here at all? Why not? Let's find out.

ANNA I sent my husband a telegram when I got here two days ago: 'DEAR NIKOLAI, ARRIVED SAFELY. HOTEL MARINO COMFORTABLE. WEATHER MIXED. DOING A LOT OF WALKING. GET SONIA TO SHAMPOO ALL THE UPSTAIRS CARPETS.'

His reply came this morning: 'I MISS YOU SO BADLY. BUT IT WILL BE A WONDERFUL BREAK FOR YOU. IT WILL MAKE A NEW WOMAN OF YOU. ENJOY IT. I WILL JOIN YOU JUST AS SOON AS I CAN GET AWAY. ALL MY LOVE TO MY INFANT. NIKOLAI.'

He was forty then. I could have been his 'infant'. And I could see his quiet earnest eyes as he wrote the words – he thought that being his infant must make me feel so assured. And even though the panic to get away from Pargolovo had already lost some of its urgency now that

9

I was here, the words 'my infant' animated that restlessness again and I had to keep telling myself that yes, Yalta would restore me, give my life some calm again, show me how much I had to be grateful for. Or at least reconcile me to what I had settled for.

GUROV You just missed the Hussars. Trying to quicken the blood for battle.

Pause.

He's a handsome little fellow.

ANNA Yes.

GUROV Is he a bit spoiled?

ANNA She.

GUROV (*to dog*) I beg your pardon.

ANNA Birthday present from Nikolai, my husband.

GUROV Very nice. (*aside*) Nikolai! An octogenarian with a bulbous nose – and a drip. (*to Anna*) Has she a name?

ANNA Not yet.

GUROV Very intelligent eyes. Understanding. May I give her a biscuit?

ANNA If you wish.

GUROV Here, girl. (*Withdraws his hand quickly.*) Hey, I'm only being agreeable.

ANNA She's nervous.

GUROV I'm not going to harm you. (*Pause.*) First time in Yalta?

ANNA Yes.

GUROV You'll be back. I come every year; part holiday, part work. (*Pause.*) I'm an accountant in a bank. (*Brief *pause.*) **Although I did my degree in philology.** (*Brief pause.*) **One hundred and seventy years ago.** (*Brief pause.*) **I'm not the most brilliant banker in Moscow. Have you been to Oreanda?**

ANNA **Sorry?**

GUROV **Oreanda – the waterfall. Almost an hour from here. Well worth a visit. There's a train every –** (*He breaks off suddenly, leans into her and speaks very softly, almost conspiratorially.*) **Don't look now; but there's a young man over there on your right. Pink cravat, white shoes. See him?**

ANNA **Yes?**

GUROV **Watch what he's slipping into his coffee.**

ANNA **Sugar?**

GUROV **Liquid heroin.**

ANNA **He's not!**

GUROV **Don't stare.**

ANNA **How do you –?**

GUROV **Had to be taken down from the top of the cathedral spire last Sunday. Before Vespers. They say his wife ran off last month with a cavalry officer.**

ANNA **God!**

GUROV **One-armed. Tragic story. And do you see that frail little creature in the satin dress – looks as if she's about to die?**

ANNA **Where?**

GUROV **No. Further left.**

ANNA **The black dress?**

GUROV She's in charge of the elephants in the Moscow Zoo.

ANNA That little white-haired lady with the –?

GUROV And the husband, the enormous man with the grey beard? (*Examines his nails.*) He knows you're talking about him.

ANNA I'm not –

GUROV (*loudly*) They expect some rain this afternoon. But it is that time of year, isn't it? (*softly again*) At least twenty-five stone weight. Too much brandy. Once the principal dancer at the Kirov.

ANNA That man was a ballet –?

GUROV Known in those days as Il Folletto. The Elf. Italian. She's German. They got married while they were still at college – just like me. And each has refused to learn the other's language; so that when they want to communicate, they write notes to one another.

ANNA They don't!

GUROV In broken English.

ANNA I think you're trying to make a –

GUROV Look. She's passing him a message now.

ANNA So she is.

GUROV He's reading it. Shakes his head. Disapproves of whatever it is she has said. Passes it back to her.

ANNA Yes.

GUROV Strange way to talk, isn't it?

ANNA Wait a minute –!

GUROV Eventually their vocal chords will atrophy.

ANNA That's the bill she handed him! (*Laughs.*) Their coffee bill!

GUROV (*innocently*) Is it?

ANNA Yes! She's putting her money on top of it!

GUROV You're absolutely right.

ANNA You are taking a hand at me!

GUROV No, no. Just playing the Yalta game.

ANNA The what?

GUROV I'll explain it later. I'm going to Oreanda tomorrow to say goodbye to the waterfall. Come with me.

ANNA Oh, I couldn't –

GUROV And bring the charming lady along and we'll baptize her up there in the silver water. What will we call her?

ANNA My husband will make that –

GUROV Yalta! What about Yalta?

ANNA A dog called Yalta?

GUROV Why not? Always remind you of here. By the way, I'm Dmitry Gurov. From Moscow. And you are –?

ANNA I . . . I'm Anna Sergeyevna. From Pargolovo.

GUROV Italian?

ANNA (*laughs*) Pargolovo is four miles north of Petersburg.

GUROV Pargolovo? It's three miles south of Rome. I think in real life you're a tenor in an Italian opera company. We get a lot of them in Moscow. (*softly*) See that man eating an ice-cream? He claims to be an illegitimate son of Queen Victoria of England. He's probably right. She had nineteen. (*loudly*) I'll pick you up at the Marino at ten and I'll have you safely home in time for dinner. You never got your coffee! (*He jumps to his feet.*)

ANNA It doesn't matter.

GUROV Maybe the coffee waiters are on a coffee break. I'll find out. Would she turn up? Perhaps. With her cranky little mongrel. And if she doesn't . . .? (*He shrugs indifferently.*)

ANNA What a strange man. One hundred and seventy! (*Laughs.*) Forty, maybe? And married? Said so, didn't he? Probably two or three children. Could be grown up by now. Not a bit like a banker – or a philologist; whatever a philologist looks like. Should ask him that. Happy nature? Not sure. For all his joking there's something . . . urgent about him.

GUROV Curious word, 'conquest', isn't it? 'I made another conquest last night.' Militaristic ring about it; maybe even a hint of violence. I'm not squeamish about it but it's a word I never used. I suppose because I've never thought of the women I've had over the years as trophies. More like companions in adventure – exciting adventures – delightful companions – light-hearted, soufflé adventures. Yes. That's how it always begins. It's an unacknowledged game, too. Of course it can become complicated; and then a bit difficult; and then maybe even a little frightening; and that's when you resolve never to become entangled again. But the beginning is always . . . joyous. And who can resist that? Why should it be resisted? (*loudly*) Isn't it an impressive waterfall?

ANNA What?

GUROV (*shouts*) Isn't it wonderful?

ANNA Yes.

GUROV It looks silver, doesn't it?

ANNA It's frightening.

GUROV A thousand gallons of water crash down there every thirty seconds.

ANNA It's a bit overwhelming.

GUROV Where's Yalta? (*to dog*) Come here and see this. (*to Anna*) She's frightened by the noise. And she's not dying about me. (*softly*) Nor I about her. (*to Anna*) Let's move back a bit. When is your husband going to join you?

ANNA As soon as he can get away.

GUROV Away from what?

ANNA His work.

GUROV What's his work?

ANNA He's a clerical officer in the office of the district council – I'm wrong – in the municipal office. (*Laughs.*) One or the other. Isn't it awful – I'm never sure which.

GUROV Shame on you. Anyhow, if he comes before I leave, we'll have to bring him up here.

ANNA You're leaving tomorrow, aren't you?

GUROV I think I'll stay on for another few days. We haven't explored the gardens. Haven't been to the casino. And on Friday night we're going to meet the Theodosia ferry. (*suddenly very softly*) D'you see that barefoot boy at the railings? Beside the woman in the green shawl? He has just lifted her purse from her handbag.

ANNA How do you –? (*She slaps his arm playfully.*) Will you stop that! Come on. We'll miss the train.

GUROV Thank you for coming with me today.

ANNA Yalta – Yalta – come on, girl – come on.

GUROV Who are you calling?

ANNA Yalta! We have just baptized her! My dog!

GUROV What dog?

ANNA My dog. There.

GUROV (*slaps her arm playfully*) Will you stop that! You know there's no dog there.

ANNA At your feet. There. Touch her. You are a very silly man.

GUROV Yes.

ANNA We're going to miss the train.

GUROV The next day we explored the municipal gardens. The following night we went to the casino, where I swaggered a little – stupidly; and lost more than a little. She was . . . prudent. And two days later, on the Friday night, we went down to the harbour and watched the arrival of the Theodosia ferry with its lights dancing and expectant.

ANNA Why did I think he was strange? He wasn't at all strange. Just an ordinary man. And considerate. And generous. And funny! God! He would say something altogether absurd and you would look at him and his face would be almost solemn. I hadn't laughed so much in years. And yet at times he would withdraw into himself and you felt that – what? I don't know – you knew there was a great loneliness in him.

GUROV I had never seen her so at ease or so happy as that night at the harbour. Or indeed so beautiful; with that unique beauty that youth endows. And in front of all those new, expectant arrivals we kissed. Yes. Without embarrassment. Then I took her hand and we went back to the Marino Hotel and up to her room. (*Pause.*) It has to be said that she locked the damn dog in the closet and the bastard scratched at the door all night long. It has to be said, too, that the next morning was . . . turbulent. Tears. Regrets. Contrition. The usual. She actually did say, 'You'll never ever respect me again.' Just a little disappointing.

ANNA (*crying*) Why should you? How could you? You picked me up in the square, didn't you?

GUROV Anna, you –

ANNA To you I'm just another street woman. How many more have you had since you came here?

GUROV I have the utmost respect for you.

ANNA And what you know nothing about and of course care nothing about is that I'm married to the most wonderful man who is kind and honourable and adores me.

GUROV Why wouldn't he?

ANNA And I have betrayed that honourable man and I have degraded myself.

GUROV Anna –

ANNA What I have done is so wrong – no, not wrong, evil, evil. I am an evil person.

GUROV Shhh.

ANNA If you could see your eyes: you despise me and you're right to despise me. Oh my God, why did I ever set foot in this corrupt place!

GUROV And the emotion was genuine. Completely. Maybe a shade . . . theatrical. But no question of fakery. The poor child did think she had become – thankfully she didn't use the words but they wouldn't have been inappropriate to the way she was feeling – 'a fallen woman'. Yes. Remarkable.

ANNA (*calmly*) All I could see were Nikolai's quiet, earnest eyes, those beautiful earnest eyes. They weren't accusing; weren't even reproachful. They just gazed at me and asked, 'Why, Anna? Why?'

GUROV Then she threw her arms around me and hugged me fiercely as if I could rescue her from herself. And I noticed how lank her hair hung round her face and how those pert little features had gone so slack. And I realized suddenly that she was only a few years older than my daughter.

ANNA I wanted so much to feel him hold me and hear him say in that gentle voice of his, 'Anna, my infant, my infant.' I needed that assurance so badly.

GUROV We got through that morning somehow. Of course I told her I loved her, as indeed I did. And finally the sobbing stopped and the fear went out of her eyes and somehow I even coaxed a laugh from her. Then we had lunch in Verner's Restaurant – mussels with garlic stuffing, done in a white wine. We both had the same. Excellent. Then a pleasant walk along the promenade. Had we had an established routine, you could have said we were back to normal.

She takes his arm and leans into him and speaks very softly, almost conspiratorially.

ANNA **Look at the pair across the street. Don't stare! See them?**

GUROV I see them. And that's my role.

ANNA Where is his left hand?

GUROV What?

ANNA His left hand – where is it? – can you see it?

GUROV I see a man in a grey –

ANNA But no left hand visible. And why not?

GUROV I see a staid couple enjoying a brisk –

ANNA The beast! Oh my God! In broad daylight!

GUROV What are you talking –?

ANNA She's trying to walk normally, but how can she? God!

GUROV Are you telling me he's –?

> *She whispers quickly into Gurov's ear – then explodes with laughter. He laughs too, and stares at her in pretended shock and amazement.*

Well, aren't you a naughty child!

ANNA I swear!

GUROV Very naughty.

ANNA But I'm right, amn't I?

GUROV Absolutely!

ANNA Look at her face! And the beast believes that if he keeps looking away from her, then nobody could guess what – (*Again she leans into him to whisper a further comment; but breaks off suddenly in panic.*) Yalta! Oh my God! Dmitry –

GUROV What?

ANNA Where's Yalta?

GUROV Isn't she there at –?

ANNA She's gone!

GUROV She's not gone. We'll stand –

ANNA Oh God, my darling birthday present. (*She begins calling the dog and dashing frantically around.*) Yalta! Yalta! Where is she? Oh God, Dmitry – she's been stolen – she's lost – she's run away! Yalta! Where are you? Yalta? You weren't watching her!

GUROV She can't be lost, Anna.

ANNA Where is she then? Yalta!

GUROV She must be around here somewhere.

ANNA You know she's not. Why didn't you mind her? Yalta! She's wise – she'll head for home. She is wise, isn't she? She'll go home to the Marino. Don't stand there, Dmitry! You keep an eye on the far side of the street and I'll search this side. Oh my God, what will I tell Nikolai if she's not in the hotel, if I have lost her?

GUROV She was right: the wise Yalta had made her way home. There she was up in the bedroom, sitting possessively on the bed.

Anna whips the dog up into her arms.

ANNA Oh my darling, darling, darling dog! Kiss me – kiss me. And again and again! (*to Gurov*) Look at how wretched she is. (*to dog*) You're right to be ashamed of yourself. But all is forgiven, forgotten, my little sweetheart. Kiss her, Dmitry – yes, kiss Dmitry, my darling. And never run away from me again – d'you hear? Never! Never! Look at that little tail wagging like mad. Isn't she just beautiful?

GUROV (*looking at Anna*) Yes. Indeed, yes. Very beautiful. Happiness all over the place.

So we pulled over the curtains and didn't go out again until it was time for dinner. And this time we were circumspect: we didn't lock the beast in the closet.

ANNA You're early. I didn't expect you for another hour.

GUROV I've got a cab waiting at the door. This morning we'll go across to Alushta to see the old Byzantine church there. It has the finest mosaic dome in the Crimea.

ANNA I've just got a telegram from Nikolai.

GUROV From –?

ANNA Nikolai. My husband. He has to go into hospital. A serious eye infection. He wants me to come home immediately. He sounds frightened.

GUROV Ah.

ANNA So I'm taking the overnight express.

GUROV Of course.

ANNA Tonight.

GUROV Yes.

ANNA Just as well I'm going, isn't it?

GUROV Yes?

ANNA Nikolai being sent to hospital – people call that fate, don't they? Will you see me off?

GUROV When does the train leave?

ANNA Seven-thirty.

GUROV Of course I'll see you off.

ANNA It is all for the best, isn't it?

GUROV (*on the train, briskly*) I think that's everything. The bed seems comfortable and the place is warm. Not too warm, is it? Your cases are up there. Where's your hatbox?

Anna holds up an imaginary box.

Good. Yalta can sleep on that mat. And there's your coffee-flask and croissants. And should you decide in the middle of the night that you don't want to see Pargolovo for another few days – I still think you made that up –

ANNA What?

GUROV Pargolovo.

ANNA That's where I live, Dmitry.

GUROV So you say. But even if you do, it's in Italy. You're going in the wrong direction.

ANNA Four miles north of Petersburg.

GUROV Sorry. Three miles south of Rome. Check when you get there. Anyhow, I was going to say that should you decide during the night that you don't want to go to Italy, pull that cord, and –

ANNA Just look at me for a moment, Dmitry, and let me look at you. (*Pause.*) No, don't kiss me, please. You know I'm never going to see you again – ever.

GUROV Anna –

ANNA But I will always love you – always.

GUROV And I will always –

ANNA Shhh. You don't have to make any declarations. Really. It would have been better if we had never met. Indeed it would. But we did meet and now my life can never be the same again. There's the second bell. Go,

Dmitry – (*He moves towards her.*) **No, please, darling, please, please** . . . **'Bye.** (*She turns away quickly.*)

GUROV The night had turned chilly and the platform soon emptied but I felt I ought to stand there until the train was out of sight. Express trains take a very long time to build up speed, I discovered. I hadn't my gloves with me and my hands were quite cold. And my feet. Autumn had arrived. The season was certainly over.

What did I feel? As if I had woken up; emerged from a sweet trance; returned from another charming adventure. A light-hearted adventure – it was that indeed. With a very sweet adventuress. And all the more agreeable because it had come to an end before the complications began and things became difficult. That was always a bonus.

But already in my mind the texture of the thing was changing. The little adventure – how long did it last? – a week? – ten days? – however real it may have seemed at the time, it was already losing that reality and beginning to drift into the category of . . . 'imagined'. But there was always something elusive, something impalpable about it, wasn't there? Did it happen at all? I began to think – truthfully! – I began to wonder, had I made it all up!

Maybe it was no more actual than the fictional lives I invested the people in the square with. (*He warms to this intriguing speculation.*) Now this was a subtle game; sly almost. There is no silver waterfall at Oreanda.

What?

None. And there never was a Marino Hotel.

You're joking.

The Theodosia ferry was a ghost ship. No municipal park; no promenade; no town square.

No town square?

All a fiction. All imagined.

23

Oh come on!

Was there even – could it be thought even in a sly
game – was there ever an Anna?

Oh, God, shame on you!

But was there?

That's unfair to her and to you.

Is it?

Of course there was an Anna, a beautiful Anna, an
exciting Anna, even though it does require a little effort
to recall that excitement. And that's unfair too. You
remember that excitement well. You remember that
excitement very well indeed . . . well, don't you? So no
more of that cheap game, that ugly game.

You're right.

You're a callous bastard, you know that?

I do know that.

So just shut up.

Very well.

But there was one element I was happy to consign
to the imagined. The damned dog was definitely make-
believe. Definitely never any Yalta.

ANNA Nikolai was a month in hospital. Then, when he
came out, he got an infection in the other eye and had
to go back in again. So for nine weeks I was alone in the
house with Sonia, the maid. It was a bleak time. The
snow had come early. It was almost an hour's walk to
the hospital every day. And I was anxious about Nikolai
because he was worrying himself sick about his job
and about money but most of all in case those quiet,
earnest eyes might lose their sight altogether. I had to
keep assuring him that they wouldn't. He had become
so dependent on me, as if we had switched roles. He
usually cried when visiting time was over.

Dmitry was with me all the time. But his presence had
different manifestations and different levels of intensity.

Sometimes I wouldn't see him for days; only the echo of his voice; and I'd strain to hear was he calling me. Or maybe a quick memory of the way he'd pronounce 'Theodosia' or summon a waiter – 'When you find a second.' Sometimes I could hear him moving around upstairs and I'd wait at the bottom of the stairs for him to come down. Sometimes he sat at the far side of the stove, reading a novel or doing his bank books; and when he remembered me, he'd look across at me and smile quickly. And sometimes he'd come up behind me stealthily and enfold me in his arms and whisper into the back of my neck, just below the hairline. And when he did that, I was flooded with such a great happiness that I would have collapsed if he had let me go.

It was a strange kind of living; knowing with an aching clarity that I would never see him again – ever; and at the same time being with him always, always, happily always in that ethereal presence. There were times when I thought I mightn't be right in the head. But I suppose what was happening to me was that I was becoming somebody altogether different.

GUROV Something peculiar happened to me over the next two months. Moscow had become intolerable – Moscow that I loved. And the work in the bank was so meaningless that I had to frogmarch myself through the routine of every day. Found myself doing things I would never have done, just to escape from the house and the sullen silence and the children demanding help with their homework. I joined a tennis club! In November! Played cards three nights a week. Accompanied a colleague to his weekly musical society evenings and endured his amateur friends playing Bach and Handel. With such enthusiasm! And with apparent pleasure, for God's sake!

But back to the peculiar thing, the very peculiar thing. Remember my sly game? Well, it . . . inverted itself. Or else my world did a somersault. Or else all reality turned itself on its head. Because suddenly, for no reason that I was aware of, things that once seemed real now became imagined things. And what was imagined, what I could imagine, what I could recall, that was actual, the only actuality. The bank, colleagues, home, card games, they all subsided into make-believe – they were fictions, weren't they? And the only reality was the reality in my mind. And that was the reality of the Marino Hotel and the silver waterfall and the town square which was the heart of Yalta. And, of course, the total reality of Anna.

So I began to live only in her presence, only in the environment that was hers. In the whisper of her breath. In the music of her laugh. In the balm of her voice. In the solace of her hands. So that when I knew in mid-December that I had to go to Pargolovo, it wasn't an impetuous decision. It was the most natural thing in the world to do.

ANNA I began to fill my weeks with small delights, exquisite little treats. Well, expectations really. And I plotted them with great care, indeed with cunning. It wasn't at all a game, a child's make-believe. No, no. It was a rehearsal for what was certainly going to happen.

On Friday afternoon, when Nikolai has gone for his check-up and Sonia is down at the laundry, at exactly four o'clock there'll be a knock at the door. Three crisp taps. I'll have a quick look in the hall mirror and then I'll open it. And there he'll be, with his straw hat and his quirky smile, and he'll say, 'Will you get a move on? The ferry's about to leave.'

And on Saturday week next, on my way to the butcher, we'll meet at noon under the town clock. Ever since I came to Pargolovo the hands have been frozen at ten; and he'll say, 'Look at that, Anna. You're two years late, for God's sake!'

And in tomorrow's post there'll be a letter from him. I'll tell Nikolai it's from my sister, Irena. It will have all the plans for our elopement to the Crimea and the house we'll have there and the whitewashed rooms and the sea-blue dishes on the dresser and the trees we'll plant and the walks we'll take. He knows blue is my favourite colour.

Yes. They were rehearsals.

The three taps didn't come. No rat-tat-tat. And he wasn't waiting under the frozen clock. And there was no letter about the sea-blue dishes. But those weren't big disappointments. Weren't disappointments at all. Only postponements of the complete happiness that had to come.

Gurov grabs her from behind. She is alarmed and totally confused.

GUROV **Anna.**

ANNA **What? – Who? –**

GUROV **Isn't it Anna Sergeyevna?**

She wheels around and sees him.

ANNA **Oh my God!** (*Pause. Softly*) **Oh my God.**

GUROV **I had to come.**

ANNA **Dmitry?**

GUROV **Dmitry – yes.**

ANNA **Oh my God.**

GUROV (*rapidly*) **I found out where you lived and I went to the house but I couldn't knock so I walked the streets for the past three hours in the hope that I would see you and I did, I did, I couldn't believe it, but there you were –**

ANNA **You've got to go.**

27

GUROV (*slowly*) – looking exactly as I knew you would – no, more beautiful. Much, much more beautiful –

ANNA What are you doing here? Listen to me! You can't stay! For God's sake, go!

GUROV And your skin smells the same and your hands and –

ANNA Where are you staying?

GUROV Where am I what?

ANNA Staying – staying! How long have you been here?

GUROV I'm in the Railway Hotel.

ANNA Oh God, this is awful. I knew I'd never see you again. I knew that.

GUROV But I'm here.

ANNA I'm out to buy paraffin.

GUROV Look at me.

ANNA We need paraffin for the bedroom lamp.

GUROV Look at me, Anna.

ANNA When are you leaving?

GUROV I'm going to kiss you.

ANNA The street is full! You've gone mad!

GUROV Just once.

ANNA People – people, for God's sake, Dmitry. No, no, please, Dmitry – go now – please go now before –

GUROV Only once.

ANNA You can't – you can't! People everywhere. Please, Dmitry. I'll come to you in Moscow next –

GUROV **Just one kiss.**

ANNA **Oh my God – Moscow, that's a promise – oh my darling –** (*She throws her arms around him and kisses him quickly.*) **I must go – Moscow, I swear – I'll write to you at the bank – it'll be early next month – oh my love, my love –** (*She kisses him again, holding his face in her hands.*) **I'm going now – oh my God, Dmitry –**

GUROV **And you're right about Pargolovo.**

She stares blankly at him – what is he talking about?

ANNA **Am I?**

GUROV **It isn't in Italy.**

ANNA **Yes.**

GUROV **No. It is in Russia.**

ANNA **Is it?**

GUROV **It's here.**

ANNA **Oh my God.**

GUROV **I was wrong.**

ANNA **No, no – Moscow – a promise. I swear, my love.**

GUROV **Moscow.**

She turns away quickly.

ANNA **I went to him in Moscow every two or three months. As often as I could. Nikolai believed I was going to see a gynaecologist. I would check into the hotel and send a porter around to the bank with a message that I had arrived. 'Il Folletto is in town' – that was our code. Dmitry's idea. Just a joke. And he would come to me that night. And in the morning I would go back to Pargolovo.** (*suddenly remembering*) **Yes, Nikolai's**

eyesight improved a lot – well, got no worse. He wore
dark glasses all the time and went for long walks with
Yalta. And to make his job easier his superior switched
him from municipal work to district council work – or
from district council work to – (*impatiently*) whatever.
Their concern for him . . . flattered him. I think he just
pretended to believe in the gynaecologist.

GUROV I had never led a double life before and it
was surprising how simple it was – at one level. My
public life continued as usual: work, acquaintances,
family, clients, holidays; fully conventional; altogether
transparent; and a total deception.
   Then there was the other life with her: tempestuous,
ecstatic, tortured and thrilling in its secrecy. That life
took over my entire being and gripped me in its mad
eddy. This is my true life, I thought, and in a way it was.
   But of course these categories – public and private,
deceptive and authentic – they are never as distinct as
we think. Because the authentic life has its own little
deceits within it and the deceptive life has its own little
authenticities. And the two categories bleed into each
other. So that a time can come when you can barely
distinguish between them. I didn't think that was a
confusion on my part. Just an acknowledgement of
things as they are. And I did love her. Oh yes. I had
never loved anyone like that before.
   Why are you crying?

ANNA **Give me a moment.**

He takes her in his arms.

GUROV **Shhh.**

ANNA **Can't stop. Just stupid.**

GUROV **There's a special perfume off your hair tonight.**

30

ANNA Our lives are in ruins, Dmitry.

GUROV Why are you so upset today?

ANNA We hide from everyone. We lie all the time. We live like fugitives.

GUROV You are such a beautiful fugitive.

ANNA And we're never going to escape. How can we? Neither of us is ever going to be free. And I love you so much, so much. No, I don't just love you – I worship you. Oh, Dmitry, my darling, you will love me always, won't you?

GUROV She believed she did worship me. She believed she would always worship me. And for the first time in my life I had come close to worshipping somebody too. But how could I tell her that this would come to an end one day? Indeed it would. But if I had told her, she wouldn't have believed me.

He releases her. They stand back to back, facing in opposite directions, holding hands.

ANNA You will love me always, Dmitry?

GUROV Yes.

ANNA And I will love you always.

GUROV I know that.

ANNA We are so lucky. Do you appreciate how lucky we are? How many people do you know have had such happiness as we have had? We have been such a . . . blessed couple, haven't we?

GUROV Yes.

ANNA I do believe that. Blessed.

GUROV Yes.

ANNA At moments like that – and we had so many, so
many of them – at moments like that I was convinced
we would find a solution to our predicament. No, not
a solution – why not a divine intervention? Yes, a
miraculous solution would be offered to us. And that
release would make our happiness so complete and so
opulent and . . . for ever. But I knew that until that
miracle happened, we would have to stumble on together
for a very long time; because the end was coming even
though it was still a long way off. But the drawing to a
close had already begun and we were now embarked on
the most complicated and most frightening and the most
painful time of all.

GUROV **Kiss me, Anna. Please.**

*They kiss. Bring up the exuberant military music in
the background.*

The End.

THE BEAR

a vaudeville
by Anton Chekhov

Anton Chekhov was twenty-eight when he wrote *The Bear*. It is a young man's play, simultaneously pushy and tentative, fastidious and crude, technically derivative but already sending out early signals of that distinctive Chekhovian voice. It was a very popular play. It provided him with an income for so many years that he referred to it deprecatingly, defensively, as *The Milch-Cow*.

When the play was first produced, in 1888, he shied away from classifying it publicly, a puzzling reticence he practised all his life. (Not one of his plays is called a tragedy. He referred coyly to *The Seagull* and *The Cherry Orchard* as 'comedies'. He described *Three Sisters* as 'a drama in four acts'.) Privately he called *The Bear* 'a joke', 'a mangy little vaudeville', 'all tra-la-la', 'a piffling little Frenchified vaudeville'. He wrote to his poet friend Yakov Polonsky, 'Just to while away the time I wrote a trivial little vaudeville in the French manner.' He was always skilled in the technique of deflecting scrutiny.

But the word 'vaudeville' persists. It is a theatrical category that no longer exists. But in the late nineteenth century those *pièces en vaudeville* were hugely popular. When their energy began to dim they found a second wind on the variety stage. There they were called sketches. And perhaps that is how we should look at *The Bear*, as a vaudeville/sketch. Its ambition is to hold our attention briefly, to entertain us, and to make us laugh at people whose over-the-top behaviour barely disguises their terrors and confused hopes. But *The Bear* engages for another important reason: it is an early trial piece by the man who reshaped twentieth-century theatre.

Brian Friel

The Bear (after Chekhov) was first produced, with
Afterplay, in the Gate Theatre, Dublin, on Tuesday,
5 March 2002, with the following cast:

Elena Ivanova Popova Flora Montgomery
Luka Eamon Morrissey
Gregory Stepanovitch Smirnov Stephen Brennan

Director Robin Lefèvre
Designer Liz Ascroft
Lighting Designer Mick Hughes

Literal translation by Úna Ní Dhubhghaill

Characters

Elena Ivanova Popova
a young and attractive widow

Luka
Elena's frail and ancient manservant

Gregory Stepanovitch Smirnov
mid-forties; very physical and very energetic;
landowner and ex-soldier

*The action takes place in the drawing room
of Elena Popova's comfortable country house.
A very hot afternoon in the summer of 1890.*

*Elena Popova sits on a couch and reads a book. Since
the death of her husband a year ago she has immersed
herself in the role of mourning widow: she is dressed
entirely in black, she speaks very softly, and she carries
her grief with resignation and fortitude. Luka enters,
staggering under the weight of a basket of logs. He
carries them to the stove and builds them round it.*

LUKA Who wants a fire on a hot day like this? Nobody
wants a fire on a hot day like this. So why am I lugging
in these logs? Because that's what you do every day. You
fill the baskets with logs and stack them round the stove.
Habit, that's why. (*He straightens his aching back.*) And
habits can injure your body. Habits can kill you in the
end, madam.

ELENA (*not listening*) Yes?

LUKA You really should be outside. Must be the hottest
day of the year. (*Laughter off.*) D'you hear them – the
cook and the chambermaid. (*He goes to the window.*)
They've picked all the gooseberries and now they're
starting on the blackcurrants. (*Calls.*) Dasha! Pelagheia!
Can I give you a hand?

*We cannot hear Dasha's ribald reply. But both girls
laugh raucously. Luka is embarrassed before Elena.*

That's naughty, Dasha! (*to Elena*) Saucy young one, that
Dasha. Too forward for her own good. Even the cat's
enjoying himself. Look.

43

ELENA Sorry? (*She puts her finger on the place where she stopped reading.*)

LUKA The cat. Sauntering up and down the verandah and pretending he's not eyeing the birds.

ELENA I'm trying to read, Luka.

LUKA I could put a chair out under the lime tree and you could read out there.

ELENA You know very well I will never set foot outside this house again.

LUKA Madam –

ELENA How often do I have to say this to you, Luka? My life is over. He is buried in his grave and I have buried myself within these four walls. We are both dead. (*She resumes reading.*)

LUKA With respect, madam, I can't listen to chat like that. Yes, your husband's dead. God's will be done; may he rest in peace. And you have mourned him – indeed you have – for twelve full months. But now it is time to stop mourning. It is time to begin living again. When my wife died, God be good to her, I grieved for exactly nineteen days. You remember Olga, madam, don't you? Deeply pious woman; such a proper woman. Wasn't nineteen days about right for Olga?

ELENA Luka –

LUKA Because if you keep on mourning like this it will become just another habit. You'll do yourself great damage.

ELENA Now may I –? (*Resumes reading.*)

LUKA I'm sorry, madam, but I have got to say what –

ELENA Luka –

44

LUKA Look at your neighbours – the best in the world – people who love you! And you'll neither call on them nor invite them here. A new regiment arrived in the town last month – handsome officers – band concerts – great dress balls every Friday night. That's where you should be, dancing yourself dizzy, not sitting there getting paler and reading *novels*, for God's sake. You're a very attractive woman. You're young. You're energetic. Will you still have that energy in ten years' time? Will you want to dance the night away then? I care so much for you, madam. Please don't let your life slip through your fingers.

ELENA You mean well, Luka. But I must insist that you never speak to me like that again.

LUKA Madam, all I –

ELENA Never. The moment Nikolai Mikailovitch passed away, I made a solemn vow that I would mourn him for the rest of my life and never again look at the light of day. When Nikolai Mikailovitch passed away, my life disintegrated; all that survived of me was my love for him. And I will demonstrate how absolute and how resolute that love was. And his spirit will have to acknowledge that steadfastness. Yes, yes, yes, it was no secret that he was often cruel to me – and – yes – unfaithful to me – I knew you always knew. But I will be faithful to him for ever. I will show him what true love really is.

LUKA But, madam, how can you show him if he's not –?

ELENA And it's not all that hot, Luka. Light the stove.

LUKA I know what we'll do! Masha Polena Andryeevna was to have come out of hospital today. She's your godmother, isn't she? I'll harness up Toby and Giant and we'll go to see her and bring her some fresh fruit.

45

ELENA He was fond of Toby, wasn't he? Always Toby he chose when he was going visiting those city friends of his. He was so handsome on Toby, wasn't he? – so distinguished, such authority. And how well he knew that. Oh Toby, Toby – the things you must have seen. See that he gets an extra bag of oats today.

LUKA Yes, madam.

An urgent ring on the doorbell.

ELENA (*agitated*) Who's that? Whoever it is, I'm not seeing anyone.

LUKA Yes, madam. (*He exits.*)

ELENA (*calling*) Nobody!

Raised voices off. Elena goes quickly to the mantelpiece, looks in the mirror, and swiftly and adroitly adjusts her hair and blouse. Her eye then falls on Nikolai's photograph.

I will show you how I can forgive and how resolutely I can love. Just you watch. You must be so ashamed of yourself. I shut myself off from every human contact, totally faithful only to you, and there you are, still looking beyond me with your slithery eyes and your weak smile and your –

Luka enters. He is frightened.

LUKA A man, madam.

ELENA Well?

LUKA A man looking for you.

ELENA Send him away.

LUKA I said you weren't receiving.

ELENA I'm in mourning, Luka.

LUKA I told him all that.

ELENA Close the door on him then.

LUKA He's a substantial man, madam, and my back isn't all that –

ELENA I will not see him.

LUKA Very urgent, he says.

ELENA Get rid of him.

LUKA He pushed me aside. He's already in the dining room. Madam, here he –

Enter Gregory Smirnov.

SMIRNOV (*to Luka*) Go and water my horse. You're about fit to carry a bucket of water, aren't you? (*He bows to Elena.*) Gregory Stepanovitch Smirnov. Landowner and retired lieutenant of artillery.

ELENA Do you usually burst your way into people's houses?

SMIRNOV Unpardonable. You're right. I apologize. But I am desperate.

ELENA (*to Luka*) See that Toby gets those oats now.

Luka is reluctant to leave her alone.

I'm fine, Luka, thank you.

Luka leaves.

(*to Smirnov*) Well?

SMIRNOV I knew your late husband. He sometimes bought his hay from me. My sympathy, madam.

ELENA Thank you.

SMIRNOV I can see you are in very deep grief. So I'll be brief. Shortly before he died, he got a very large supply of hay from me. He hadn't the money to pay for it when it was delivered. So he sent me this memorandum of debt. (*Holds up a paper.*) Twelve hundred roubles guaranteed within three months. That was over a year ago.

ELENA So?

SMIRNOV I need that money now. Urgently.

ELENA If Nikolai Mikailovitch owed you money, of course you will be paid.

SMIRNOV I can't tell you the relief that –

ELENA When my steward comes back from the town. He should be here the day after tomorrow. Come back then and we'll discuss the matter. (*She deftly takes the paper from his hand.*) May I?

SMIRNOV I haven't made myself clear. I must have the money today, madam. If I don't have another instalment with the Agricultural Bank first thing tomorrow morning, they will repossess my estate and kick me out on the street.

ELENA Nor have I made myself clear. I have no money in hand today. When my steward comes back the day after tomorrow, he and I will examine this (*sheet*) – and pay you what we owe you, if we owe you.

SMIRNOV 'If we –'?

ELENA Besides, my husband is barely a year dead and I'm in no mood to concern myself with your petty affairs.

SMIRNOV My house and land repossessed – petty? Thrown out on the shit-heap – petty?

ELENA Language, sir! The day after tomorrow.

SMIRNOV The day after tomorrow I'll be a bankrupt.

ELENA The day after tomorrow.

SMIRNOV Pay me what you owe me.

ELENA Can't.

SMIRNOV Can't or won't?

ELENA The day after tomorrow.

SMIRNOV If you say the day after tomorrow just once
more, by Christ I'll –

ELENA (*very softly, very angrily*) How dare you speak to
me like that! You burst into my house like an angry bear.
You threaten me and my servant. You demand money
and swear like a trooper. If you're not out of this house
in five minutes, Luka will fling you out.

SMIRNOV (*feigned terror*) Oh, lady, please not Luka!

Elena marches off.

Cool down, madam. I only want your roubles – that's all!
God, I'm parched. (*Looks into a press for something to
drink.*) All right, I suppose I'm sorry about your husband
and I don't want to barge in on your grief. But you could
at least have some understanding of my situation. Since
five this morning I've been going round my debtors and
pleading for what is mine, for Christ's sake. The cute
hawk Yatosevitch saw me riding into the yard and took to
the hills in his nightshirt. Old Grozdiov must have had a
premonition I was coming: went and died two nights ago.
Slippery bastard. I said that to his son and he set the old
man's dog on me. Kuritsin gave me no money but a lot
of cheek. So I thumped him. Mistake. His son's a lawyer.
And now this weepy bitch. Bad – bad – bad, my friend.
And this damned heat's no help. What did she call that
old scarecrow? (*Calls.*) Hercules! I'll have to squeeze
her harder.

Luka enters.

LUKA Yes, sir?

SMIRNOV A jug of water.

Luka hesitates: should he obey this intruder?

(*Shouts.*) Water! Are you deaf? A large jug!

Luka exits. Smirnov kicks off one of his boots and examines his ankle.

That bloody mongrel of Grozdiov did draw blood. I was right to shoot him. That stirred the wake up a bit. Need to stir this place up, too. I'll be honest with you, lady: I don't give a shit about your husband or about you and your grief. Just hand over what is mine.

Luka enters with jug of water.

LUKA Madam is indisposed. She is seeing nobody for the rest of the day.

SMIRNOV I don't want water now. Bring me vodka! (*Shouts.*) Vodka!

LUKA I'm sorry, sir, but I must ask you not to –

SMIRNOV (*shouts*) Vodka! – vodka! – vodka! Now!

LUKA (*innocently*) Did you mention vodka? Certainly, sir. (*He exits.*)

SMIRNOV The old fart isn't taking a hand at me, is he? So madam is indisposed. We'll just have to wait until madam is disposed then, won't we? (*Kicks off the other boot and goes to the window.*) Unharness the horses, Alex, and give them their oats. We're going to be here for some time. (*Spreads out in a chair.*) Indeed we are.

Luka returns with a bottle of vodka and a glass.

50

That's more like it. Off you go and play with the cat. (*Rubs his ankle.*) Bastard! That's damned sore.

As Luka is about to exit:

Hercules, who are the two skirts I saw in the garden?

LUKA The two –?

SMIRNOV (*shouts*) Scullions – tarts – broads! The maids, man, the maids.

LUKA They are in the employment of Madam Popova.

SMIRNOV (*affectedly*) Good heavens, are they now? (*normal*) What do you call the tall one?

LUKA Sir, I don't really –

SMIRNOV Black hair, wonderful thighs, two great big –

LUKA Dasha.

SMIRNOV Ah! So the old crab is alive. Well, tell Dasha that Gregory Stepanovitch Smirnov spotted her for one second in the distance and his life has taken an altogether new course.

LUKA I will inform her of that.

SMIRNOV (*as Luka leaves*) No, you won't. (*Smirnov pours a drink, knocks it back quickly, pours another. Now he wanders around the room in his stockinged feet. Stops at the mirror.*) God, I need a bath and a change of clothes. Good Christ, what an awful bloody mess I'm in. (*another quick drink*) Careful, lieutenant. Too early to get plastered. (*moving around*) Nice quarters though. Snug. Bit of style. That's what you need, Greg: style. And money.

Elena enters. She now wears a scarlet shawl around her shoulders. Smirnov holds up the bottle.

51

Vodka from Kiev. (*He sprawls in a chair.*)

ELENA (*barely controlled*) Your shouting is unpardonable.

SMIRNOV Have a nip?

ELENA This is a house of grief. Voices are never ever raised in this house.

SMIRNOV (*whispers*) I'll be a mouse. Promise. (*He massages his ankle.*) Could I get rabies from this? (*Now she sees he is not wearing his boots.*)

ELENA And you are not in some low tavern, sir. Put on your boots and leave at once.

SMIRNOV When I'm paid what I'm owed.

ELENA We've been over all this.

SMIRNOV Old Grozdiov's was the second place I called on this morning. Another bad debt. And d'you know what his bastard son did? Set his damned dog on me.

ELENA We cannot conclude our business until my steward returns.

SMIRNOV So of course I shot the bloody thing.

ELENA I have explained to you: I have no money here.

SMIRNOV Whisky drives me mad in the head but vodka makes me . . . benign. Should have shot the bastard son, too.

ELENA Come back the day after tomorrow and we'll –

SMIRNOV (*roars*) Christ Almighty, we're not back to that rant, are we? (*a little quieter*) Listen carefully to what I'm saying, woman. You owe me twelve hundred roubles. I am not leaving this house until I have it in my hand. Quite clear? (*now calm and smiling*) Tell Hercules to pick up my things in the stable. My man, Alex, will give them to him. And tell him to bring them up to the guest room. Is it in the front or the back of the house?

ELENA Never in my life have I met such an insolent, such a revolting creature.

SMIRNOV I know what's wrong with me! I haven't eaten since breakfast! I'm ravenous. Black suits you.

ELENA Insolent and ill-bred and no idea how to behave in the company of women.

SMIRNOV But you know that.

ELENA Have you ever mixed with civilized people?

SMIRNOV You should take a charge of this (*vodka*). What's for dinner?

ELENA I can't believe that there are still people like you who have no sense whatever of the civility a man should show a woman – damn it, the common courtesy.

SMIRNOV Ah-ah – language.

ELENA But clearly I'm wrong. The country's probably full of gentlemen like you with the manners of the barnyard.

SMIRNOV Careful now.

ELENA But then the army was always a breeding ground for vulgarity and coarseness and indeed plain, crude misogyny. Have you always hated women?

SMIRNOV (*trying to keep calm*) Madam, I have spent more time in women's company than you have spent saying your prayers. Married three times. Lived with ten others at different times; jilted four and was jilted by six. Fought duels over five. And all in all pleasured and was pleasured by scores of them.

ELENA Well, aren't we wonderfully experienced?

SMIRNOV I love women in my own way. Not in that
swooning, foppish, melting, bogus way you look for –
I served my time at that game. Wrote poems to a woman
once! Horse-shit! For God's sake, even campaigned for
women's emancipation! And then – suddenly – I must
have been thirty, for Christ's sake! – I saw through all
that fakery: the significant glances, the lowered voice,
the subtle perfume, the squeezed hand, the quick intake
of breath. (*great laugh*) Jesus Christ, that's the real horse-
shit! Because behind that fake discretion and those
demure eyes you women are all the same, my friend –
hard-boiled, ice-hearted, utterly selfish – crocodiles. And
tough! Oh, God, tough as a badger's arse!

ELENA Sir –!

SMIRNOV And about as faithful as a rabbit.

ELENA Hold on there –!

SMIRNOV That shawl's new, isn't it? You hadn't that on
when I arrived, had you?

ELENA Just stop there –!

SMIRNOV Nice touch. But you know that, too.

ELENA Women are more faithless than men?

SMIRNOV Not old women. Fewer opportunities.

ELENA God, you're so delicate.

SMIRNOV Accurate though.

ELENA I'll tell you about faithful, Mister Profligate Soldier.
The man I am now mourning and will mourn till the day
I die, I loved that man with every fibre of my body. He
was the only reason for my existence. I worshipped that
man the way a pagan prostrates himself before his god.
And all the years of our marriage that god of my life

cheated on me. Not occasionally, not casually, but persistently, bloody compulsively. During all the years of our marriage I put up with that treason and all that deep, deep hurt. And for all the years of our marriage, in spite of that deep hurt, I still loved him and kept faithful to him. And even though he is gone I love him still and will still be faithful to him. And I will prove to him that faithfulness and constancy still do exist in this world.

SMIRNOV (*bored*) Bravo. Have a nip?

ELENA So don't lecture me about being faithful.

SMIRNOV It's true – it does make me benign.

ELENA You . . . reprobate!

SMIRNOV Please don't shout at me.

ELENA I'm not shouting.

SMIRNOV Bellowing.

ELENA I will shout in my own house if I wish.

SMIRNOV Now you're being childish, aren't you?

ELENA And I will say just one more thing.

SMIRNOV Be brief. This is boring.

ELENA (*almost incoherent*) This is –?

SMIRNOV All this 'faithful to his memory', 'faithful till I die' stuff. Balderdash. As my mother used to say, you're a blether-skite. You don't believe a word of it yourself.

ELENA So I'm a liar?

SMIRNOV Admit it.

ELENA Get out of my house.

SMIRNOV Money first.

ELENA Out! Now! (*Shouts.*) Luka!

SMIRNOV Shouting again.

ELENA (*quietly*) Luka! (*defiantly*) Luka!

Luka enters.

Luka, get rid of this brute.

Luka stares at Smirnov, then at Elena, then back to Smirnov. He freezes at the enormity – at the absurdity – of her command. Long pause.

LUKA (*breezily*) The general opinion seems to be that this could well be one of the great years for honey. Isn't that interesting? The hot weather, I suppose.

ELENA I said throw him out, Luka.

SMIRNOV (*to Elena*) That's not fair. The poor man's almost over the hill. (*sympathetically to Luka*) Aren't you? I have a gun in my bag. Would you like me to –? (*Mimes shooting him.*)

LUKA (*terrified*) Good God, sir – please, sir – madam –! Water! Dear God, I'm going to pass out! Oh sir –

He slumps into a chair and gasps for air. Elena rushes to the window.

ELENA Dasha! Dasha! Quickly! Pelagheia! At once!

SMIRNOV (*pulling on his boots*) Yes, let's have the wonderful Dasha! (*to Luka*) We would go anywhere for her, wouldn't we, old rooster?

LUKA Could I have a drink of –?

ELENA (*to Smirnov*) I have three men working at the hay and two more cutting corn. They'll soon fling you out on your face.

LUKA Madam, please could you get me a –?

The more Elena raises her voice, the quieter Smirnov becomes.

SMIRNOV *(to Luka)* She's threatening me again.

ELENA So before they come I'll ask you just one more time: get out of this house at once!

SMIRNOV *(to Luka)* I'm ravenous, Hercules.

LUKA Sir, could you –?

SMIRNOV Do *you* know what's for dinner?

ELENA Now!

SMIRNOV Shouting again.

ELENA I am not shouting – you animal, you bully, you filthy-mouthed insolent beast.

SMIRNOV What was that?

ELENA Bear, pig, womanizer –

SMIRNOV Sorry?

ELENA Bastard – army bastard – low-life bastard!

SMIRNOV Why are you deliberately insulting me?

ELENA Because you're a beast! Because I despise you!

SMIRNOV *(barely audible)* You give me no alternative, madam –

ELENA Stop roaring at me!

SMIRNOV – but to challenge you.

LUKA Oooh!

ELENA To a duel? You're challenging me to a duel? What a gentleman you are!

SMIRNOV Pistols?

LUKA Oooh God!

ELENA Splendid!

SMIRNOV You want sexual equality, equal rights?

ELENA Excellent! I have pistols in the house.

SMIRNOV You accept?

ELENA I certainly do! Here and now?

SMIRNOV Here and now.

ELENA Perfect. Out in the old orchard.

LUKA (*staggering to his feet*) Oh madam, madam – sir, please – this madness will –

ELENA Everything's fine, Luka. The beast has got to be put down. (*to Smirnov*) Nikolai Mikailovitch has a pair of pistols in his bedroom. Give me a minute. (*She exits.*)

LUKA Sir, in the name of God I beg you not to –

ELENA (*suddenly appearing*) You have no idea how much pleasure it will give me to sink a bullet into the skull of that animal. Right (*middle of her forehead*) there. (*She exits.*)

SMIRNOV (*in amazement and delight*) Jesus, what a spirited little bitch that is!

LUKA (*grasping Smirnov's hand*) For the sake of Almighty God and His Holy Mother, I beg you, sir, I implore you to leave this unhappy house now.

SMIRNOV (*not hearing Luka*) Well! Did you ever in your life see anything like that?

LUKA Just walk out the door and the whole sorry episode will be –

SMIRNOV Where did that astonishing fury come from, Luka? What became of my mousey little nun? How did Nikolai Mikailovitch ever hold on to a tornado like that? Maybe that's what killed him! Because that is a force of nature! Did you see the flush in her cheeks, the white fury in her eyes? And did you hear her? – she wants to shoot me!

LUKA Sir, I know she doesn't mean that in any –

SMIRNOV 'To sink a bullet into the skull of that animal'! That is a biblical passion! For God's sake, what a magnificent woman! Never in my entire life have I met a woman like that, Luka! That creature is unique, Luka!

LUKA Please, sir, if you would just leave now, sir, I promise I'll pray for you every morning and every night until my maker sends for me.

SMIRNOV I have to take her down, of course; wing her at least. But, as you said, it will be a contest of equals.

LUKA I said? Sir, I never –

SMIRNOV And *you* do appreciate what you're going to witness, don't you? The final emancipation of women. And I'm so fortunate that the woman I am chosen to liberate is such a superb creation – as you put it. (*He clenches his fists and does a brief celebratory dance.*)

LUKA But, sir, I never said –

SMIRNOV (*arm round Luka's shoulder*) A secret, my friend, Luka. It *is* Luka, isn't it? Minutes after I got that final demand from the Agricultural Bank, I felt a hand on my shoulder and a voice from above said to me, 'Go forth on your journey, Gregory Stepanovitch, and stop at the house of the grieving widow because I have vouchsafed that a great joy will take possession of you there.' God's hand, Luka.

LUKA Sir, I –

SMIRNOV God's voice, Luka.

LUKA Sir, that sun is too hot for you. And the sun and the vodka, sir, together they can –

SMIRNOV And before we go out to the old orchard, Luka, there is something I want you to know: how impressed I am by your loyalty to that wonderful mistress of yours; more than impressed – moved. (*He grips Luka's hand with great sincerity.*) She is blessed. You are blessed. We are all blessed, Luka.

LUKA (*altogether confused*) Blessed, sir; blessed indeed; we are, aren't we?

SMIRNOV As for retrieving my money, Luka, what has money to do with inner happiness? Nothing!

Enter Elena with pistol case. Her manner – and Smirnov's – are now calm and matter-of-fact.

ELENA Here we are.

SMIRNOV Good.

ELENA Bit dusty, aren't they?

SMIRNOV (*offers handkerchief*) Use this, Elena. It is Elena, isn't it?

ELENA Yes. Thank you.

SMIRNOV As long as they fire.

ELENA They'll fire. This catch (*on the case*) is a bit rusty.

SMIRNOV Allow me.

ELENA I can manage. (*Opens case.*) There.

SMIRNOV Well done.

ELENA Your handkerchief.

SMIRNOV Thank you.

ELENA Soiled, I'm afraid.

SMIRNOV Doesn't matter in the least. These (*guns*) are yours, are they?

ELENA No, no.

SMIRNOV Your husband's?

ELENA My late husband's.

SMIRNOV Nikolai Mikailovitch?

ELENA That was his name.

SMIRNOV Was he a good shot?

ELENA Why do you keep talking about my late husband?

SMIRNOV Sorry.

ELENA Should tell you: I've never fired a pistol in my life.

SMIRNOV Never?

ELENA Never.

SMIRNOV Are you serious?

ELENA So you'll have to show me how to use it.

SMIRNOV A pleasure.

LUKA (*frantic*) *I'll* get the men in from the fields! A curse has fallen on this house! (*Shouts.*) You are both out of your minds. (*He rushes off.*)

ELENA What's the matter with him? Luka!

SMIRNOV May I take this? (*case*)

ELENA Of course.

SMIRNOV He doesn't like to see us bickering, I suppose. (*Opens case.*) Handsome.

ELENA Are they?

SMIRNOV Very handsome. Smith and Wesson movement; conventional duelling pistols. Triple-action extractor.

ELENA Yes?

SMIRNOV Well balanced, too. Nice engraving on the barrel and that ivory finish is very unusual.

ELENA It is pretty.

SMIRNOV Worth ninety roubles a brace at least. Fine. Let's get started.

He stands behind her, his arms around her, and puts a gun into her hand.

Now, grasp it around the – You're not left-handed, are you?

ELENA No.

SMIRNOV Then switch over.

ELENA Right hand?

SMIRNOV That's it. You hold the gun in the right hand and your left hand gives it support. Now pull that lever back.

ELENA Like this?

SMIRNOV Well done. That's called cocking the gun. Now you aim it – like this. A little higher. Good. And hold your head back a little. Little more. (*His face is now buried in her hair. Softly*) Jesus Christ!

ELENA Sorry?

SMIRNOV Perfect – beautiful. Now stretch your arm full length – that's it – (*Pause as he gazes at the back of her head.*)

ELENA Well?

SMIRNOV Wonderful. Now pull back the hammer.

ELENA I've done that.

SMIRNOV Have you? So you have.

ELENA So what next?

SMIRNOV Next you press the trigger with your finger – your hand is so tiny –

Pause.

ELENA I'm pressing. Go on!

SMIRNOV Don't pull it. Just press it firmly. Great. You're superb at this –

Pause.

ELENA And that's it?

SMIRNOV That's it. Take your time when you're aiming. The important thing is to keep calm. And you've got to keep that hand from shaking.

ELENA My hand isn't shaking.

SMIRNOV Is it not?

ELENA Yours is.

SMIRNOV Right. I think you've got the basics.

They separate. He picks up his gun.

ELENA The old orchard is behind the stables – (*She moves towards the door.*)

SMIRNOV Before you go. I've got to warn you –

ELENA Are you coming?

SMIRNOV I won't aim at you.

ELENA What are you talking about?

SMIRNOV I will fire into the air.

She stands in front of him and looks closely at him.

ELENA He's funking it! Yes! Look at those flinching eyes!

SMIRNOV I'm not –

ELENA You're the one who threw down the challenge, Lieutenant, now you're going to see it through. I'm sinking a bullet up there – remember? I'm not going to be deprived of that delight. Oh, no, sir.

SMIRNOV You're right. I have lost my nerve. Look – my hand is shaking.

She examines his face more closely.

ELENA You're a liar, too. Why won't you fight?

SMIRNOV Because . . . Damn it, how can I fight you when I like you so much?

ELENA He likes me! Listen to him! The man says he likes me!

SMIRNOV And I mean that with –

ELENA He breaks into my house – intrudes on my sacred grief – demands a fortune from me – drinks my vodka – tries to seduce my maids – uses filthy barrack language in my presence – threatens to shoot my manservant – bellows, screams at me – and then says he likes me. How would he behave if he disliked me!

64

SMIRNOV In fact I think maybe I'm in love with you.

ELENA Get out of here.

SMIRNOV Never met a woman like you in all my days.

ELENA I think I hate you.

SMIRNOV So perceptive, so spiritual, so sensual, so vital. You are truly magnificent. (*He moves towards her.*)

ELENA Another step and I'll shoot.

SMIRNOV And those azure eyes that sing to me. And that hair that caressed my face. And that pliant body that melted into my arms. Oh, God, yes, I'm in love with you! I'm so in love with you.

ELENA I think you're deranged.

SMIRNOV Am I?

ELENA Leave now. Please.

SMIRNOV And maybe lose you for ever? You know nothing about me – I know that. What can I tell you? From decent enough people. A substantial estate about fifty-seven miles to the north-west. Reasonably well stocked. I have some good brood mares and a saw-mill that –

ELENA 'Substantial' – 'well stocked' – you're bloody broke!

SMIRNOV Is money everything? I enjoy hunting, the odd drink, meeting old colleagues, a flutter now and then – Jesus, woman, marry me!

ELENA Language!

SMIRNOV Will you?

ELENA You promised me a duel! Keep your word!

SMIRNOV Of course I will – anything you want –
anything in the whole world – just name it. What am
I saying? I'm ranting – I know I am. I love you as I've
never loved anyone in my whole life.

ELENA You were married three times.

SMIRNOV And look at me now – drunk with your subtle
perfume – swooning before that incredibly beautiful face.
Without you I know I cannot live.

ELENA You jilted four others.

SMIRNOV How could I have loved them when I never
knew what love meant until I met you? I liked them, I
suppose. Maybe I had some affection for them. What has
that got to do with what I feel now? Because I'm
orbiting the world in a whirl of madness – now my heart
has exploded into a million pieces – now I'm beyond
words, outside logic, free of all reason. Now I am light
and air and hovering at the edge of heaven. You have to
marry me – now!

ELENA Why?

SMIRNOV Don't – and you'll regret it until the day you
die. Look at me: swooning, abject, obsequious, pleading.
Marry me!

ELENA But I hate you.

SMIRNOV Marry me!

ELENA You're bullying me, you – you – you – dog-
assassin!

SMIRNOV Marry me!

ELENA Never! Never ever!

*Pause. He assesses what she has said. He picks up his
cap and goes towards the door.*

You know you're a bully. And foul-mouthed. And unfit for any civilized society.

SMIRNOV 'Bye.

ELENA (*shouts*) Go on, then! Back to your crumbling estate and your mountain of debts and your drunken gambling sessions with your friends. And tomorrow morning the Agricultural Bank will fling you out on top of the shit-heap where you belong –

SMIRNOV 'Bye.

ELENA – and that will be too bloody good for you, you bastard!

SMIRNOV 'Bye.

ELENA And don't come back here the day after tomorrow or any other day because there's no welcome for you here.

SMIRNOV (*real concern*) You're shouting again.

ELENA I am not.

SMIRNOV 'Fraid so.

ELENA I am not shouting.

SMIRNOV Need to watch that. You're far too young to be getting cranky. You should be out there in the sunshine laughing with the two girls. Is there no fun in your life?

Pause.

ELENA You're right. I'm becoming a shrew – a bitter, soured old . . . Tartar. It's showing in my face. Look.

He looks closely at her.

The corners of my mouth have got so tight, and look at the lines here. Good Christ, what an awful bloody mess I'm in!

He takes her in his arms.

SMIRNOV No, no, no, no, no –

ELENA I should be left alone.

SMIRNOV You a shrew? You are the light of –

ELENA Keep away from me.

SMIRNOV Can't do that.

He kisses her hair, her neck, her shoulders. They both speak dreamily.

ELENA Oh, Gregory, please go now – please. It is Gregory, isn't it?

SMIRNOV Gregory. Never going to leave you.

ELENA Do I hate you?

SMIRNOV Never.

ELENA Take this (*gun*) away. My hand is numb.

SMIRNOV Never ever.

ELENA My mind is numb. I'm numb all over, Gregory.

SMIRNOV I adore you.

ELENA You aren't a beast, are you?

SMIRNOV Adore you.

ELENA If you go now, you'll come back the day after tomorrow, won't you?

SMIRNOV Adore you.

ELENA Promise me you will.

SMIRNOV Oh my darling –

ELENA Oh Jesus Christ –

Prolonged kiss. Then Luka enters with an enormous hay-fork. He is agitated and very determined.

LUKA Madam, I am now ready to – (*Breaks off when he sees what is happening.*) Almighty God and His Holy Mother –

ELENA Tell them in the stables, Luka – no oats at all for Toby today.

Quick blackout.

The End.

AFTERPLAY

Author's Note

I called this piece *Afterplay* because it revisits the lives
of two people, Andrey Prozorov and Sonya Serebriakova,
who had a previous existence in two separate plays.
Both plays were written by the same author one hundred
years ago.

These two people came from very different fictional
backgrounds and we meet them again now approximately
twenty years after their previous fictional lives ended.
Sonya was then in her twenties and Andrey in his early
thirties. Now re-animated and re-imagined they are
middle-aged. They cannot escape their origins, of course;
those experiences that their creator furnished them with
are still determining experiences. Part of Andrey is still
an only boy, confused, motherless, reared in a remote
provincial town by a domineering father and three
restless sisters. Sonya is still wrestling with a difficult
estate and is still as deeply and as hopelessly in love with
the local doctor as she was all those years ago. But they
have had new experiences in the twenty-year interval.
And what interested me was what those experiences
might be and how they might blend into and adjust
those earlier lives.

Had I created these two characters in the first place
I would feel free now to reshape them as I wished. But
they are not mine alone. I am something less than a
parent but I know I am something more than a foster-
parent. Maybe closer to a godparent who takes his
responsibilities scrupulously. So when I consider the
complex life Anton Chekhov breathed into Sonya and
Andrey one hundred years ago I believe that that life

can be carried forward into this extended existence provided the two stay true to where and what they came from. That means that the godfather has to stay alert at all times to the intention of their first begetter.

Afterplay was first produced, with *The Bear* (after Chekhov), in the Gate Theatre, Dublin, on Tuesday, 5 March 2002, with the following cast:

Andrey John Hurt
Sonya Penelope Wilton

Director Robin Lefèvre
Designer Liz Ascroft
Lighting Designer Mick Hughes

Characters

Sonya Serebriakova

Andrey Prozorov

A small run-down café in Moscow in the early 1920s.
Night-time.
   Sonya Serebriakova is the only customer. She has a
forgotten glass of tea at her elbow. She is in her forties.
Her hair is grey and she is wearing reading glasses. She
appears to be a controlled, determined and efficient
woman. Her table is littered with official-looking
documents and maps, which she scrutinizes eagerly. But
it is obvious that they have baffled and exhausted her.
   Andrey Prozorov enters. He is in his late forties. He
has a bowl of soup in one hand, a plate of brown bread
in the other, and in his arms he cradles a violin case,
which he hugs to his chest. Under one arm he carries a
canvas carrier bag. He wears a shabby coat over a very
shabby dress suit. Because of his shyness he smiles a lot –
a very unreliable guide to what he is really thinking.
   As he passes Sonya's table Andrey pauses, smiles and
nods his head again and again.

ANDREY Hello again.

Sonya looks up. She does not recognize him.

SONYA (*coolly*) Good evening. (*She returns to her*
documents.)

ANDREY You have your hands full.

SONYA Sorry?

ANDREY We met last night. We shared that table. Last
night.

SONYA Yes?

ANDREY We had a wonderful chat, too. About chapped lips.

SONYA About –?

ANDREY Chapped lips and chilblains. Fascinating.

SONYA (*suddenly remembering*) Of course! The man with the very talented family!

ANDREY Oh God! Don't remind me.

SONYA A very gifted daughter and an absolutely brilliant son.

ANDREY Please don't embarrass me.

SONYA Of course I remember. Forgive me. Sit down – sit down.

ANDREY When I came in the door I recognized you instantly –

SONYA (*offering a chair*) Here.

ANDREY – by the back of your head.

SONYA (*puzzled*) Yes?

ANDREY Looks as if we have the place to ourselves again tonight.

SONYA And you've been to rehearsals again.

ANDREY Non-stop since early afternoon.

SONYA At the Opera House?

ANDREY At the Opera House.

SONYA You always rehearse in dress?

ANDREY German conductor – Munich – obsessed with formality. (*Moves on.*) Well – enjoy your tea.

SONYA And you enjoy yours.

ANDREY Soup.

SONYA Better still.

ANDREY And brown bread.

SONYA Is it fresh?

ANDREY Oh yes: it's brown, you see.

SONYA (*puzzled*) Ah.

ANDREY The same witch at the counter – did you notice her? She snarled at me when I paid her.

SONYA She bites, too.

ANDREY (*uncertainly*) You're joking, aren't you?

SONYA Won't you sit down?

ANDREY No, no. You're up to your –

SONYA (*gathering papers*) I'm so sorry. This stuff has my head addled. Please do.

ANDREY I'm interrupting you. And you have –

SONYA You're not interrupting me at all but you *are* making me very uncomfortable just standing there.

ANDREY Sorry. Yes. Thank you. Yes. (*Sits.*) Sonya, isn't it?

SONYA Sonya.

ANDREY Yes.

SONYA Sonya Serebriakova.

ANDREY How do you do.

SONYA Andrey?

ANDREY Andrey.

SONYA Yes.

ANDREY Andrey Prozorov.

SONYA How do you do.

ANDREY Cabbage soup.

SONYA (*to bowl*) How do you do.

ANDREY Sorry?

SONYA (*laughs*) Being giddy. I told you the head's a bit –
(*Her hands flutter in the air in illustration.*)

ANDREY Tired, are you?

SONYA A little. An early night tonight. I'm getting the
first train home tomorrow. (*remembering*) You're right:
how in God's name did we get on to skin rashes?

ANDREY You said you had some herbal cures.

SONYA I don't. Why did I say that? It couldn't have been
fascinating, was it?

ANDREY You're right. How could it have been? (*He takes
off his coat and begins eating.*) Forgive me. I'm ravenous.

SONYA We talked about living alone, too.

ANDREY So we did.

SONYA And how to cope with it.

ANDREY Yes.

SONYA We agreed there were times when it was just a
little . . . difficult.

ANDREY It must be.

SONYA (*puzzled*) We did agree it was, didn't we? How
long is your wife dead?

ANDREY I really don't know. Isn't that disgraceful? A long time. Seventeen years? Maybe more. And your uncle?

SONYA Nineteen years next September the ninth, God be good to him. And I'm ashamed to say we got a bit emotional last night. No, you didn't. I did.

ANDREY Did you?

SONYA (*briskly*) I think you made the better choice. That soup looks good.

ANDREY Lukewarm.

SONYA Take it back then.

ANDREY To that gorgon? Oh, no, I –

SONYA (*grasping bowl*) If you won't, then I certainly –

ANDREY No, please, no. It's beautiful lukewarm.

SONYA Is the bread fresh?

ANDREY Perfect. It's brown, you see.

SONYA (*puzzled*) Of course. And how were rehearsals tonight?

ANDREY We played well, I think. But my feet and legs are sore. Can you imagine what it's like standing in the one spot for over six hours? Agony!

SONYA The orchestra rehearses standing up?

Pause.

ANDREY No, it doesn't actually rehearse standing up. What happens is this. When you sit on a hard chair for a very long time, especially in the string section, your bottom goes numb – if you'll pardon me. So what you have to do every so often is leap to your feet and slap your thighs to quicken the flow of blood throughout your whole body. But then – then – then – with all that standing on your feet – *they* begin to go numb. So that after five or six hours' rehearsal you're numb all over because there are all these perplexing demands on your circulation system and it can't decide which deserves its attention more – feet or bottom. So what it does is, it does nothing at all. So that, after a day's rehearsal, you have hardly any feeling anywhere. If you'll pardon me.

SONYA Why especially in the string section?

ANDREY Why what?

SONYA You said you go very numb especially in the string section. Why?

   Pause.

ANDREY Because in every orchestra the string section are always big wine-drinkers. And notorious gossips.

SONYA I have no idea in the world what you're saying, Andrey.

ANDREY Yes, I'm explaining it very –

SONYA Go back to the beginning: it is *La Bohème* you're rehearsing?

ANDREY *La Bohème.*

SONYA At the Opera House.

ANDREY Right.

SONYA An opera by Puccini, you told me last night.

ANDREY Yes.

SONYA Born in Lucca in 1858.

ANDREY So it said in the paper.

SONYA Is he still alive, this Puccini?

ANDREY Oh, no. I wouldn't think so.

SONYA Could be, couldn't he? –

ANDREY I'm sure he's dead.

SONYA Do you know he's dead?

ANDREY No.

SONYA Then don't be so gloomy. The conductor is a bully from Munich, the orchestra is efficient, and Mimi herself is thrilling.

ANDREY Have you seen her picture on the poster? Radiant. And she's only nineteen!

SONYA (*tartly*) Good for her. And it's going to be a huge popular success.

ANDREY How do you know?

SONYA You said so yourself.

ANDREY Did I? I don't think I could have –

SONYA When does it open?

ANDREY Tomorrow night.

SONYA I'd love to see it but I have to be home by tomorrow night. Pity.

ANDREY It's going to be a thrilling night. I'm very excited by it all.

SONYA Enthusiasm – that's better!

ANDREY Why the surprise? I'm a great enthusiast. The girls – my sisters – they say it's my nature: effervescent, they say. How did your meetings go today?

SONYA Good. Great. Couldn't have been more satisfactory.

ANDREY I'm delighted.

SONYA The bank in the morning and all afternoon with the Ministry of Agriculture people. Couldn't have been more helpful, the Agriculture people.

ANDREY That sounds good.

SONYA It does, doesn't it? The bank has come up with a remarkable idea. What they propose is – what they're strongly urging me to do is – no, I'm not going to bore you.

ANDREY Please. I'm interested.

SONYA Well, they say I've got to cut out the crops we've always grown – wheat, rye, corn, barley. That's finished. Too risky and too difficult for a woman on her own. And what they insist is –

ANDREY The Agriculture people?

SONYA The bank, actually. No, of course they don't insist – what they advise me to do is plant the estate with trees.

ANDREY The entire place?

SONYA Trees everywhere.

ANDREY How many acres?

SONYA All three hundred. I was wrestling with all this documentation when you came in. Very complicated; and everything seems to have been agreed on so suddenly. But I will get on top of it. All I need is a little time. And they assure me this will provide me with an adequate income. Ultimately. Probably just as I'm dying. Could be very exciting, couldn't it? – afforestation.

ANDREY Enthusiasm – that's better!

SONYA And a complete break with the past – that would be such a release, wouldn't it?

ANDREY A lot to be said for it.

SONYA There is, isn't there? (*formally*) 'And trees aren't just magnificent things in themselves. Of course they adorn the earth and affect the climate. But they also inspire in us a sense of awe and offer us a source of spiritual sustenance.'

ANDREY (*applauds*) Bravo!

SONYA Not mine. A very dear friend of mine. A passionate tree-man.

ANDREY Have you talked to him about the proposal?

SONYA He would be all for it, I know. (*quickly*) Look at this rubbish – titles, overdrafts, mortgages. Baffling, isn't it? And I used to be so skilful at all that stuff. As good as any accountant. Don't look sceptical. I was. And Uncle Vanya was happy to let me run the estate because I *was* so competent at it and because he knew in his heart he was incompetent.

ANDREY What does running an estate entail?

SONYA I hired the men; rented the machinery; haggled in the market; kept the accounts. Everything. For God's sake, I even did the books for our two neighbours for years and years.

ANDREY Just like my Natasha – my wife, Natasha. Wizard at accounts, too. (*Pause.*) God have mercy on her.

SONYA Amen to that. No, I'm not saying I was a wizard.

ANDREY Natasha was really no wizard either; not at all.

SONYA But I was very competent.

ANDREY That's closer to it.

SONYA Then two things happened almost simultaneously. My father died in Moscow and his very young widow, my stepmother, came to live with us for a year. The beautiful, the exquisite Elena. Fair, elegant, charming and maybe – who's to say – maybe a little heartless. Exactly the same age as myself. But so beautiful. And poor Uncle Vanya fell madly in love with her. For the first time in his life. Utterly, hopelessly. And he was twenty-five years older than her. But she *was* so beautiful. I can't tell you. Exactly the same age as myself. And the second thing that happened – of course it was because of his sudden dementia – was that sweet Uncle Vanya decided one morning that running an estate was a man's work. He must take over all those burdens. And that's what he did. With all the doggedness and crude determination that only an indecisive man can muster. And the estate began to collapse and our money problems became serious and grew greater every year until . . . this. Poor man. He knew he had made a complete mess of it but he wouldn't let me take over again. And the beautiful Elena had gone. And he became sullen and cantankerous and obsessed with trivial things. The doctor said the stroke was probably brought on by anxiety.

ANDREY Probably.

SONYA Collapsed at breakfast. A calm harvest morning. Never regained consciousness. I sent word to Elena – she was holidaying in France. But she didn't come. Vanya wouldn't have known her even if she had.

ANDREY God rest him.

SONYA But what was so very happy for me was that, over the three weeks he lay there, I watched his face shed every trace of that anxiety and that ugly obstinacy; and I saw him return to the benign, bumbling Uncle Vanya he once was, that gentle creature who used to bang the table and shout, 'I'm positive I'm right!' – with no conviction whatever.

ANDREY Just you and he alone on the estate?

SONYA He was the only family I ever knew.

ANDREY So you told me.

SONYA And watching his life ebbing away I knew that a core part of me was going with him. As you say, God rest him.

ANDREY He lasted just three weeks?

SONYA Three weeks and a day. We sat up with him every night, Michael and I, one on each side of the bed.

ANDREY Michael?

SONYA My very dear friend; the tree enthusiast; the family doctor.

ANDREY Ah.

SONYA After the servants had gone to bed and the house was silent. It was a difficult time but I knew it was a privileged time, too. And that vigil we kept together, Michael and I, one on each side of the bed, not speaking, just being together there, even though he was often so drunk he would doze off, I knew that those were the most serene and most fulfilled days of my life.

ANDREY Michael what?

SONYA Astrov. Dr Michael Astrov. A man with a vision; and close to saintliness; and not always sober. (*briskly*) Have you trees?

ANDREY Oh yes.

SONYA Why didn't you say so? A plantation owner – the very man to advise me.

ANDREY I'll tell you all I can.

SONYA How many acres have you got?

ANDREY We have two birches at the bottom of the garden.

SONYA 'Two –!' (*Laughs.*) Oh my God.

ANDREY Ridiculous – yes, so ridiculous.

SONYA Enormous birches, I hope!

ANDREY We're not farming people.

SONYA Is it even a big garden?

ANDREY Quarter of an acre. We were never farming people. Father was an army man. I was born here in Moscow. I was only four when his regiment was posted to Taganrog, almost eight hundred miles south of here. That's where I've lived all my life.

SONYA He had his own regiment?

ANDREY Yes. General Prozorov. A man of such determination. Admirable.

SONYA So you travelled five hundred miles just to do this opera?

ANDREY There isn't much work for a violinist in Taganrog. I do some teaching but I'm not a great violinist. I travel when I get the chance.

SONYA All the same, that is real enthusiasm. Good for you.

ANDREY Can I get you fresh tea?

SONYA No thanks.

ANDREY That must be cold.

SONYA It's fine.

ANDREY Forgive me for last night, Sonya. God knows what rubbish I talked about the children.

SONYA Bobik is a doctor and Sophie is an engineer. You were so proud of them.

ANDREY An untruth, I'm afraid. Bobik gave up medicine after a year. Sort of a vagrant now, I hear; last seen here in Moscow. Sophie never qualified either. Worked for a while with a building firm and now lives somewhere in Kazakhstan, I think.

SONYA Do they write?

ANDREY No.

SONYA They have their own lives to lead.

ANDREY They have, haven't they? Natasha used to say – Natasha, my wife, their mother – she used to say that my sisters spoiled them because they had no children of their own. But they weren't spoiled children. Natasha was just being naughty because the girls never really made *her* welcome in the house. Considered her a little . . . graceless. Her country vigour made them . . . uneasy. What about some soup?

SONYA I don't think so.

ANDREY Soup and bread?

SONYA Nothing for me.

ANDREY It's brown.

SONYA And fresh – I know. Nothing.

ANDREY (*to his plate*) Hello, fresh brown bread. (*Laughs.*) I can be giddy, too, you know.

SONYA How many sisters have you?

ANDREY Just two now. Poor Masha died fifteen years ago.

SONYA She must have been young?

ANDREY Thirty. Shot herself with father's old revolver.

SONYA Oh God.

ANDREY But for some years before, she had already left us; gone in on herself. A love not requited, as they say.

SONYA I'm sorry, Andrey.

ANDREY A lieutenant colonel. Married. Poor Masha was married, too; to a local teacher. The affair was . . . tempestuous while it lasted. Then the lieutenant colonel was posted to Moscow and just vanished from her life. She wrote to him every day, then every week; but she never heard from him. Just vanished from her life. It was then she began to withdraw from us all. (*briskly*) But the other two girls – I can't tell you how courageous and how intelligent those ladies are. But I've always been surprised by one thing – especially since they are such intelligent girls. And what surprises me is – (*Breaks off.*) I'm talking far too much.

SONYA What surprises you is –

ANDREY That they believe that the life they lead in Taganrog isn't their real life at all, not their authentic life. Isn't that silly? Their life in Taganrog is a sort of protracted waiting time for the real life that has still to happen. And they are convinced that that authentic life is available here, in the Moscow of their childhood, a Moscow they haven't seen for over forty years! Isn't that peculiar?

SONYA I don't think so.

ANDREY Of course you do!

94

SONYA I'm sure Masha believed absolutely in a Moscow.

ANDREY Maybe. But I know, too, that they will never leave Taganrog; because they know in their hearts that the Moscow dream-life is just that – a dream. But I suppose some people live like that – in perpetual . . . expectation.

SONYA Indeed they do.

ANDREY Peculiar, isn't it?

SONYA You've said so already. It's obvious you love them, your sisters.

ANDREY They love me, too, even though I'm a bit of a failure; because I'm a bit of a failure. I was expected to become a great academic! Can you imagine? – me! But I do know that life has eluded those intelligent girls. To live your life in a waiting room – that's not strange?

SONYA No.

ANDREY That's not how you live your life, is it? What stupid dreams are you waiting to be realized? (*suddenly embarrassed*) Sorry – forgive me – I beg your pardon – I don't mean to – (*Rises.*) I'm going to get some tea. Sure?

She waves her hand to indicate she wants nothing.

If she tries to bite, I'll give you a shout. (*He goes to the door and stops.*) I must stop calling them girls – my sisters. They're in their late forties, for God's sake!

He exits. She looks after him for a long time. Then she swiftly opens her bag, takes out a vodka bottle and pours a drink into her tea-glass. She drinks that quickly. Then she pours another drink and puts the bottle back into her bag. He returns with a glass of tea.

SONYA You didn't call. Don't tell me she has fallen for you? God, that would be worse, wouldn't it?

ANDREY I'm afraid I told you a little fable last night.

SONYA A little –?

ANDREY No, not a fable; not a fable at all. A small fiction – a trivial little falsehood. Maybe just a tiny fabrication that –

SONYA (*firmly*) What are you saying, Andrey?

ANDREY That Natasha, my –

SONYA Your wife – I know.

ANDREY You're so right. My wife. Natasha. She isn't dead. It was very wrong of me to say she is. And I said, 'God have mercy on her.' That is *very, very* unlucky.

SONYA She left you.

ANDREY How did you know? Yes; went off with the chairman of the local district council. Creature called Protopopov. Bobik and Sophie were eight and ten at the time.

SONYA What became of them?

ANDREY Natasha, my . . . Naturally Natasha wanted to take them with her. But Protopopov wouldn't have them near him. So she had to leave them behind. Can you imagine the wrench that must have been for her?

SONYA I suppose so.

ANDREY Oh, yes; devastating. I was working in the council at the time. Dispatch clerk, second class. Of course I had to get out.

SONYA The children were fortunate to have their aunts to look after them.

ANDREY We are all fortunate. Because after Natasha left, I'm afraid I became a little . . . disturbed. Life became a little too difficult for me. For almost ten years. The girls were invaluable then. But that's another story.

SONYA Have you seen Natasha since she walked out?

ANDREY Frequently. She lives just outside the town! Splendid big mansion on the bank of the river. Always had a weakness for little. . . ostentations. But I really am alone – if you don't count the girls – sorry, the middle-aged women. Look at the time it is! And you have an early start.

Long pause as Sonya observes him. Then she suddenly produces the vodka bottle and holds it over his tea glass.

SONYA A drop?

ANDREY What's this?

SONYA Vodka.

ANDREY You're joking.

SONYA From Kharkov. Best in the country.

ANDREY What a bold, bold woman you are!

SONYA Will I put it in the tea?

ANDREY No – no – no – no.

SONYA Just a little?

ANDREY Oh my God.

SONYA One drop. (*She pours.*)

ANDREY Enough!

SONYA More?

ANDREY Stop – stop – stop!

SONYA Taste it.

He takes a mouthful, holds it there, then swallows it.

ANDREY Indeed.

SONYA Wonderful stuff? (*She pours a drink for herself.*)

ANDREY Yes – yes – yes.

SONYA Are you a vodka man?

ANDREY Don't enquire.

SONYA You are?

ANDREY Once upon a time. Off it for years.

SONYA Totally?

ANDREY One small drop.

She pours a drink. He throws it back.

This is good.

SONYA Isn't it?

ANDREY Am I a vodka man? For almost ten years vodka dominated my life, for God's sake. Andrey Prozorov? Taganrog's own tearaway. Drinking, gambling, carousing, fighting, roistering all round the town. For almost ten years I had Taganrog terrorized, for God's sake. (*Pause.*) Another confession to make.

SONYA Let me guess. Taganrog wasn't terrorized.

ANDREY How did you know? I was just the town drunk and utterly harmless. (*Extends his glass.*) May I?

She pours him another drink.

Suddenly the evening has become a most special evening. At least it has for me. What a clever woman you are. (*vodka*)

SONYA It's a help.

ANDREY And now a toast. To your very special friend, Michael Astrov.

SONYA Very special.

ANDREY A man with vision and close to saintliness and – what?

SONYA Not always sober.

ANDREY Isn't that a wonderful combination! Most interesting. (*toast*) To Michael.

SONYA To Michael.

ANDREY And to your new forest. May it be a source of spiritual sustenance.

SONYA He does believe that.

ANDREY And to Sonya Serebriakova herself, who is happily and elegantly here again tonight.

SONYA Thank you.

ANDREY You know – I hoped you might be.

SONYA Did you?

ANDREY I have to get those chilblain cures from you, don't I?

SONYA And to Andrey Prozorov who reminds me of Uncle Vanya in so many ways.

ANDREY Do I?

SONYA And can I pay him a greater compliment? And finally to Giacomo Puccini.

ANDREY May he rest in peace.

SONYA You're so damned stubborn. That's the Vanya thing in you, too. To the huge plantation at the bottom of your garden.

ANDREY Careful.

SONYA Sorry.

ANDREY To bankers with chilblains and civil servants with chapped lips. (*They both laugh.*)

SONYA And to two most agreeable nights –

ANDREY Yes!

SONYA – when I might have been sitting in my shabby digs and brooding on a future that terrifies me.

ANDREY Terrifies? What are you –?

SONYA Frightens, then. Only frightens – that's all. We'll see. All is not lost. If I could just muster a little extra courage . . . (*Throws back a drink. Then, with sudden animation and resolve*) I'll stay over another night! I'll go and see your opera! Now there's a brainwave!

He sits there staring at her, his face completely blank. Pause.

ANDREY Yes?

SONYA What d'you say? Who's waiting for me at home? A doting housekeeper and a drunken yardman. And they don't even know I'm away! One extra night and damn the cost. What d'you think?

ANDREY Yes?

SONYA I've got to see this radiant Mimi that you keep drooling over. I may even get a peek of the top of your head in the orchestra pit – no, the back of your head! And who knows – maybe I'll spot Signor Puccini pacing up and down outside the theatre. Settled! An opera ticket that costs the earth and an extra night I can't afford! Wonderful! Is that not courageous enough for a start?

ANDREY Yes.

SONYA And you won't see me at the end of the night.
That's a special time for you and your musician friends
to wind down – I know that. So I'll go straight home.
Here. Put your address on that (*paper*) and I'll write and
tell you how brilliant you all were.

ANDREY (*not moving*) Yes.

SONYA You're afraid you're going to be responsible for
me. You're not. I promise. (*Now she reads his mood.
Pause.*) You think it's an idiotic notion. I should go home
in the morning – that's what you think, isn't it? Not very
subtle, are you? Of course you're right. The great
brainwave seems silly already. Of course I'm not staying
over. Back to the empty house and the dripping eaves and
the rusting machines in the yard. Anyhow, I suspect that
the great Puccini isn't the next Bach and the child Mimi
sounds like a precocious tart and your conductor a quack
from Düsseldorf or Hamburg or wherever. Quacks always
try to hide behind strict formality. (*Holds up her glass.*)
And this is new; well – newish. And no help at all really.
I know that. But I have it under some sort of control.
Can't end up like my old yardman, Pietr, can I?

ANDREY Why don't you talk to your friend, Michael?

SONYA What about? Bees? Damned trees? Making us all
'better' people? All this (*papers*) – the disturbing here
and now – today's grim ultimatum – that should be
sufficient to absorb me, to worry about. And of course
I am worried. Did I tell you they've repossessed that rich
farm along the river? I bought that farm myself when
I was twenty-one – yes – with the money I gathered from
rearing calves. Gone. And they refuse to give me a loan
to fence the new forestry. And, after they've done their
survey next week, will they even leave a roof over my

head, for God's sake? Of course I'm worried. But stupidly, stupidly it's not next week that terrifies me – all right, frightens me. It's that endless tundra of aloneness, of loneliness, stretching out before me. Most of the time I can summon enough courage to carry on; just about. But courage isn't sufficient any more. If I am to carry on, I will have to summon that cardinal virtue, fortitude, won't I? If I am to carry on, that *enduring* courage, fortitude, will be required, won't it? (*Pours drink.*) Just one. One tiny little drink to conclude a very agreeable night. When her lieutenant colonel walked out on her, that's what your sister, Masha, required – fortitude. Courage might have got her over his betrayal; but she needed fortitude to keep on living. And it mustn't have been available to her. Anyhow – (*Toasts.*) To tomorrow night and to a great, great success.

ANDREY Another little fable.

SONYA Sorry?

ANDREY No, not a fable at all. A tiny fiction. A small untruth. Of course I'm ashamed of all the untruths I've told you last night and tonight; but you'll agree most of them were trivial. But this little fiction about *La Bohème* is just that bit larger and probably unpardonable and you may feel that I have misled you shamelessly and you may decide that you cannot forgive me; and if you do I will fully understand that –

SONYA Andrey, what are you –?

ANDREY – although in self-defence I must say that the *La Bohème* fiction was not premeditated but came to me on the spur of the moment shortly after we began talking last night at that table over there; and when you told me that the yolk of a lightly boiled pheasant's egg was good for chilblains, for some bizarre reason it occurred to me

at that very moment – absurd, I know, absurd, absurd –
but I suddenly thought that if I said I was a violinist in
an orchestra, that would sound very grand and I might
impress you.

SONYA Andrey, are you telling me –?

ANDREY I'm not in any orchestra.

SONYA Not in –?

ANDREY We're on the street.

SONYA What does that mean?

ANDREY That's where we play. Outdoors.

SONYA Not in the Opera House?

ANDREY On the street.

SONYA Not in the Puccini?

ANDREY On the street.

SONYA You busk.

ANDREY You're right.

SONYA Oh my God. You were never in Puccini?

ANDREY Never.

SONYA Never in the Opera House?

ANDREY Buskers.

SONYA Where were you tonight?

ANDREY At Central Station.

SONYA And last night?

ANDREY The National Gallery – outside.

SONYA On the pavement?

ANDREY Yes.

SONYA Who is we?

ANDREY Ivan and myself.

SONYA He's a fiddler, too?

ANDREY Ivan plays the balalaika. Badly. Would it be a bit cheeky of us to play outside the Opera House tomorrow night?

SONYA Andrey –!

ANDREY Why not? Nobody knows of my association with *La Bohème* except you.

SONYA What association, in the name of God?

ANDREY None. You're right.

SONYA So that every detail you told me about the opera – one lie after another?

ANDREY Sorry. Began so innocently, too.

SONYA And the radiant Mimi and the bullying conductor and the efficient orchestra –?

ANDREY Little fictions.

SONYA Little –? Bloody lies! And the flow of blood to your precious bottom and feet – that was really touching, wasn't it?

ANDREY That's no fiction. That's true.

SONYA Why am I asking? What do I care? Lie away, for God's sake!

ANDREY You're right to be angry.

SONYA Angry? Why should I be angry? And that – that – that –?

ANDREY The suit?

SONYA That's what buskers wear, is it?

ANDREY I tell myself privately that it is a classical touch. Well, down-at-heel classical. You think it's not appropriate?

SONYA Yes! – no! – maybe! – what do I know what you should wear! There isn't a busker's uniform, is there?

ANDREY You think it's inappropriate?

SONYA Andrey, honest to God I don't think I know anything any more.

ANDREY Ivan wears one, too. With a purple silk cummerbund.

SONYA The bad balalaika player?

ANDREY That was hasty. Indifferent but keen. His is slightly shabbier than mine. But then he has that splendid Uzbekistan physique, you know.

SONYA No, I don't know.

ANDREY Oh, yes. Good height, broad shoulders, straight back. He carries it magnificently, Ivan.

SONYA That makes me very happy.

ANDREY Yes, he looks just splendid.

SONYA How long will you stay here?

ANDREY Another week, maybe. Then home.

SONYA But you'll be back?

ANDREY We come here every month.

SONYA In all your classical grandeur?

ANDREY You're mocking me.

SONYA Or is this monthly visit another little fiction?
I don't know what to believe any more. And I really
don't care.

ANDREY I'll tell you why I come to Moscow.

SONYA And for all your experience you're a damned
bad liar, too.

ANDREY Bobik is in jail here.

SONYA Andrey, will you, for God's sake, stop this –!

ANDREY I was with him this morning. Yes. In the jail.
He has been there almost two years. Trumped-up charge
of theft with violence. Was set up by a friend who got
off, of course. Anyhow, this busking business gives me
a chance to visit him. Pays my train fare and digs here.
No, not a fable, Sonya. No moral core at all, I'm afraid.
Just a dismal fact.

SONYA Your son, Bobik?

ANDREY I always come out of that place feeling crushed.
Although he's fortunate enough: has a job in the prison
hospital. He said to me today – joking, of course – he
said, 'I'll be a doctor yet!'

SONYA How often can you visit him?

ANDREY As often as I can afford to bribe the man who
issues the passes. Once a month maybe. I sit with him
for an hour; not that we have all that much to talk
about. Never asks about his mother, Natasha, my wife
Natasha. Strange that, isn't it?

SONYA Does she know he's in jail?

ANDREY I hope she doesn't. Why lay that anxiety on
her? He asks in detail about the girls, his two aunts. He

broke their hearts, he thinks. And he always asks for news about Sophie. She's in Kazakhstan by the way – Sophie.

SONYA So you *are* in touch?

ANDREY One short letter last Christmas. I can't quite make out what she does. Something to do with horses. Breeds them, I imagine. Married, I hope. Nine children definitely.

SONYA (*laughs*) I'm sorry. 'Definitely'!

ANDREY So she said.

SONYA Nine!

ANDREY She takes after me – effervescent. Mustn't she?

SONYA Andrey! When does Bobik get out?

ANDREY A year and a half. A lot of numb feet between now and then.

SONYA I'm sorry I was flippant about your busking.

He shrugs.

And I think the down-at-heel classical is a wonderful idea.

He shrugs again.

You should have a cummerbund, too.

ANDREY What colour?

SONYA Defiant scarlet.

ANDREY Not my colour.

SONYA Make it your colour. Small one? (*drink*)

ANDREY Very small. You have an early start.

SONYA So – no *La Bohème* for either of us?

ANDREY 'Bye, Mimi.

SONYA 'Bye, cranky conductor. Go home to Berlin.

ANDREY Munich, actually.

SONYA But you've made it up?

ANDREY Better than Berlin, isn't it?

SONYA He is German though, isn't he?

ANDREY Italian.

SONYA God. Big question: is Puccini alive or dead?

ANDREY Who cares?

SONYA Nobody. By the way, that date, 1858, is it right?

ANDREY Wild guess.

SONYA Thought so. (*Toasts.*) Thank you for your very good company.

ANDREY (*raises glass*) For yours.

SONYA This (*drink*) is the end.

ANDREY Very end.

> *She begins packing her documents and maps into a canvas carrier bag.*

SONYA (*preparing to leave*) In fact Sonya Alexandrovna Serebriakova is beginning to feel a tiny little bit woozy. So what she must do is gather her papers and tiptoe past the gorgon and lay her head on her single pillow and dream of birch trees and dripping eaves.

ANDREY Tell me about Michael.

SONYA (*quickly alert*) About –?

ANDREY Your very close friend, the passionate tree-man.

SONYA A man of vision; and close to saintliness –

ANDREY And not always sober. You've told me that.

SONYA What else? Late fifties. Average height. Quick
blue eyes. Occasionally very prickly. Not a Uzbekistan
physique, I'm afraid.

ANDREY And your local doctor.

SONYA When he's not off on one of his schemes. He
travels all the time. He must have overseen the planting
of tens of thousands of acres of trees all over the
province. Three times he has gone to Sakhalin Island to
look after the convict prisoners there during a typhus
epidemic. He sets up apiaries in remote villages and
teaches the peasants how to manage them. He believes
that, if we were all to pay just a little attention to our
environment, it would respond so warmly to that
attention and would blossom under it; and we in turn
would become better and more generous people ourselves.
And he's so right. Just a little attention is all that is
needed. I don't think he believes in God but he believes
in human perfectibility. He sometimes uses the word
holy. I think maybe he is a holy man himself.

ANDREY Is he married?

SONYA (picks up a map) The river farm I bought all
those years ago with my calf money. I told you about
that, didn't I?

ANDREY Do you love him?

SONYA They've left me with only a few fields.

ANDREY You are in love with him, Sonya, aren't you?

SONYA For twenty-three years. Desperately. Without any
hope at all. Ever since I first met him. I was a young
woman then and he had just qualified and his quick blue

eyes bewitched me instantly and for ever. He talks very rapidly and when he danced his exuberant hopes before me – all those outrageous ideas and extravagant plans – ideas I had never heard spoken before – my head went giddy with shock and delight. (*Her hands flutter in the air in illustration – as before.*) Yes, like that. And he loved me, too. I know he did. For maybe a year. Until those great social issues gradually took over his life and he gave himself over to public things. But he still comes to me – occasionally – when he remembers me – for some reason usually when he's drunk. And when he does remember me, when he does come to me and stands swaying before me and holding my face between his hands, not saying a word, just gazing into me with those quick blue eyes that are now touched with a little uncertainty, at times like that I feel we have never been apart – ever; and I feel – God forgive me – I feel that for that moment I am almost holy, too. Not much of a way to get through your life, is it?

She concentrates on her packing. He writes on a piece of paper.

Full cousins, aren't they?

ANDREY What?

She points to the almost identical canvas carrier bags.

SONYA Yours and mine.

ANDREY (*handing her a piece of paper*) That's my home address. And that's where I stay when I'm here in Moscow.

SONYA Thank you.

ANDREY When will you be back here?

SONYA God knows. Whenever all this has to be finalized. Soon, I imagine.

ANDREY Maybe within the next few weeks?

SONYA Probably.

ANDREY Would you do something for me? When you know for sure, would you let me know?

SONYA Yes.

ANDREY Just a note to that address. I can come any time that suits you. We don't usually book a pavement in advance. I would like to meet you again.

SONYA I would like that, too. Very much.

ANDREY Great! We'll have a grand dinner together. Somewhere we can't afford. Romanoff's! I have never been to Romanoff's. Have you?

SONYA Have I ever been to Romanoff's!

ANDREY Settled.

SONYA Why not eat here? I've got suddenly fond of this place.

ANDREY And the biting gorgon?

SONYA Fond of her, too.

ANDREY Here it'll be, then.

SONYA And we'll ask them to have in vast supplies of fresh brown bread.

ANDREY Careful. May I have your address?

SONYA Of course. (*She writes the address.*)

ANDREY If you'd prefer not to –

SONYA I'd love to hear from you. I really would.

ANDREY Then indeed you will.

SONYA 'Sonya –' You know my name, don't you?

ANDREY Indeed I do.

SONYA There you are.

ANDREY Thank you. I'm going to have more tea. Will you have some?

SONYA I really have to go to bed. I'm falling apart.

ANDREY I'm sure.

SONYA So. Goodnight, Andrey.

ANDREY A very goodnight to you. Sleep well. We *will* meet again very soon.

SONYA Yes. I hope we will.

ANDREY And in the meantime I'll write to you.

SONYA Please do.

They shake hands. He kisses her cheek.

Goodnight.

ANDREY Goodnight. I'll write to you tomorrow; first thing.

She hesitates at the door and returns to the table.

SONYA I told you an untruth, Andrey.

ANDREY Sit down.

SONYA No, I'm leaving. Well, a little fiction. Maybe even a little fable because maybe there is some moral instruction at the heart of it. I didn't tell you the complete truth about Elena, my stepmother.

ANDREY The exquisite Elena. Fair, elegant, charming Elena.

SONYA Yes.

ANDREY Exactly the same age as yourself.

SONYA Yes.

ANDREY And maybe a little heartless.

SONYA Did I say that? Anyhow. Two men loved Elena very much. Poor Vanya, of course. Hopelessly. For almost a year. He didn't die of love but he never really recovered from her rejection. The other man was Michael. But she was so very beautiful. He was, too. They were such a beautiful couple.

ANDREY They married?

SONYA Yes, they did.

ANDREY Have they a family?

SONYA No. Like him she spends most of her life travelling: Paris, London, Rome; wherever there are shops. And he's immersed in his own private crusade – rescuing the damned world. I suppose they meet up occasionally. All of which is of no interest to you. And the reason I'm telling you is that I won't meet you next month.

ANDREY I don't understand.

SONYA And I'd ask you not to write to me.

ANDREY Why, Sonya?

SONYA Because every so often he comes looking for me. I never know when. When he remembers me, I suppose.

ANDREY When he's drunk, for God's sake!

SONYA That's true.

ANDREY Forgive me, Sonya.

SONYA No, no, you're right. But I love him, you see. And in his own way I know he has a love for me. And now that those quick blue eyes have lost much of their

assurance, he remembers me more often. And when
he does, when he does come to me now, I believe I'm
a little more value to him. So we stagger on, within an
environment of love of sorts, offering each other
occasional and elusive sustenance. Not the most
satisfactory way to get through your life, is it? But it
is a way. Your Masha didn't think so. But I know it is.
Yes, fortitude is required. And when I summon that
necessary fortitude, as I will, practise that cardinal
virtue, then my life will begin to cohere again and I'll
live without regrets and I'll treasure whatever is offered
to me, however occasional, however elusive; and that
endless tundra of aloneness and loneliness may still
frighten me but it will have no terror for me any more.
'Bye, Andrey.

He moves towards her.

Please. (*She goes.*)

ANDREY Sonya –!

*He stares after her. Then very slowly he puts on his
coat and gathers his belongings. He finds the paper
with her address. He gazes at it. Then impetuously and
with great determination he brushes his belongings
to the side, sits down and begins writing rapidly.
Occasionally he stops to consider what exactly he
wants to say. Then he begins writing furiously again.
Slowly bring down the lights.*

The End.